EDMUND BURKE'S BATTLE WITH LIBERALISM

EDMUND BURKE'S BATTLE WITH LIBERALISM

His Christian Philosophy
and
Why It Matters Today

SAMUEL BURGESS

Wilberforce Publications
London

First published in Great Britain in 2017 by
Wilberforce Publications Limited
70 Wimpole Street, London W1G 8AX

Wilberforce Publications Limited is a wholly owned subsidiary of Christian Concern

ISBN 978-0-9956832-3-5

Printed in the UK by Imprint Digital, Exeter

and worldwide by CreateSpace

'For Your Tomorrow, We Gave Our Today.'

Part of the *Kohima Epitaph*, attributed to John Maxwell Edmonds
(1875-1958)

Society is 'a partnership not only between those who are living,
but between those who are living, those who are dead, and those
who are to be born'.

Edmund Burke, *Reflections on the Revolution in France* (1790)

Commendation from

The Rt Rev. Dr Michael Nazir-Ali

Samuel Burgess well identifies the tension between an authentically conservative view of society as based on a shared identity, history and sense of belonging and the dominant libertarianism of all major parties in the U.K. today. This latter emphasises autonomy, freedom and equality, whilst playing down the need for cultural and national cohesion. He highlights Burke's critique of contractarian liberalism which imagines hypothetical individuals prior to society, which is seen as brought about by a desire for such individuals to protect themselves. For Burke society is basic and primal and humans are intrinsically social creatures. He takes an organic and evolutionary (rather than revolutionary) view of social development in which the spiritual and moral tradition of a society must take its due part. Where the Church of England is concerned, it should help to form the moral consensus, in the light of the Christian tradition, rather than capitulating to libertarian pressure. Freedom cannot be based on the minimalist 'no harm' to others position but must also take account of our responsibilities to the rich fabric of social relations of family, friendships and communities. Autonomy, the 'general will' of the people and State supervision are not enough for a flourishing social and political order.

The libertarian views individuals as virtuous monads, whereas Christianity regards them as both in the image of God and as fallen creatures who may need restraint not only to prevent harm to other individuals but also for the sake of the common good. Social order reflects a generally ordered universe and, like it, can best be understood as teleological, that is ordered to purpose and destiny. Natural rights language can best be understood as arising from such a spiritual and moral framework rather than being a product of reason alone.

The author points out that one of the differences between the American and French Revolutions was that the former was more organically related to the British institutions and values which preceded it, whereas the latter was an attempt to radically restructure the State in the light of 'pure reason'. This leads to the idea that its values can be imposed on others because they are more 'reasonable'. This led not only to the false religion of the 'Supreme Being' but to the reign of terror in the name of freedom! As seen in subsequent history, such radical secularism does not tolerate dissent and tolerates religion only if it does not challenge the moral consensus of contractarian liberalism. If it does, it should be combated and contained like war and disease. Such liberalism assumes the validity of its is own presuppositions but they need to be submitted to as much of a critique as its critique of religion and tradition.

According to the author, Burke believed that if people recognised accountability to a higher power, this would lead them to greater restraint and respect for others. The exercise of authority would itself be seen as a vocation to be lived out selflessly, sacrificially and honestly. A proportionate combination of reason, a formed conscience and networks of relationships is more likely to lead to an enlightened and tolerant society than just the 'pure reason' of 18th century revolutionaries or their present-day counterparts. For Burke, there can be no true conservatism without religion as a basis for social obligations and no religion is true if it abdicates its responsibilities in the public square.

Samuel Burgess has given us a very insightful survey of Burke's political and social philosophy. It should be a matter of deep concern to all of us that such principled conservatism is hardly to be found on the political spectrum today. I hope that this book is read widely by Christians in politics and that this may result in a renewal of Burkean political life.

Contents

Foreword

Edmund Burke was neither reactionary nor illiberal: throughout his life he supported the liberation of Roman Catholics from civil and political penalties, and he famously laboured for many years fighting the East India Company's oppression of native Indians. Nevertheless, highly sceptical of the glittering promises of radical, revolutionary change and deeply appreciative of the costly, organic achievement over time of the institutions of responsible government, Burke was undoubtedly conservative. In his important book, Samuel Burgess performs the signal service of discovering the Christian roots of Burke's compassionate conservatism – especially those running through the common law. In doing so, he supplies Christians today with a rich intellectual resource as they strive to get the measure of the anti-patriotic, multicultural, cosmopolitan, and secularist assumptions of the liberalism that now prevails among us.

Nigel Biggar
Regius Professor of Moral and Pastoral
Theology, University of Oxford

Acknowledgements

I would like to thank Chris Insole, who inspired me as an undergraduate to undertake further academic study and introduced me to the work of Edmund Burke. His work has served as a benchmark to aspire towards. For this I am enduringly grateful. I would also like to thank Nigel Biggar, whose work has been a source of inspiration for me and exemplifies the value of insightful and comprehensible scholarship. Thank you to John Scriven whose sagacity and meticulous proof reading proved invaluable in the final stages of the book.

In the Spring of 2014 I was lucky enough to spend time as a visiting fellow at the John W. Kluge Center at the Library of Congress. I would like to offer my thanks to the Kluge Center for allowing me to use their resources and for being so accommodating during my time there. I would like to thank all the tutors and lecturers who taught me at the Universities of Durham, Cambridge and Oxford. In particular, I would like to acknowledge the contribution of the late John Hughes, who was always generous with his time and whose tutorials I never failed to enjoy.

I am indebted to John Perry, with whom I have had many helpful conversations regarding Locke's liberalism. Additionally, I would like to thank James Orr who went beyond the call of duty in proof reading my work. I'd also like to thank Joe Smith and Simon Call for their confidence in me.

In particular, I am thankful to my late grandmother Jean, for showing me the merit of hard work in the face of great adversity, without whose perseverance I would not have had the opportunities that I have had. Also, to my grandmother Antonia Burgess for showing me the importance of an unrelentingly positive attitude.

Finally, I would like to thank my mother and father for being a constant source of guidance and encouragement. I'd like to thank my brother James for putting up with me all these years. And thank you to my remarkable wife Antonia, for all of your loving support, for which I am deeply grateful.

Above all, thanks to God.

Introduction

2016 may well be remembered as the year in which the political orthodoxies of the West were up-ended. In both the United Kingdom and the United States a landmark popular vote signalled a rejection of the political establishment. On both the left and the right there was a rejection of a set of beliefs, derived from the liberal tradition, that have been increasingly dominant in both Europe and America over the last thirty years.

In this book we shall look in detail at the development of the liberal tradition and how it is defined by the idea that individuals are autonomous, free and equal. We can also identify a series of associated beliefs which follow from this idea: a rejection of patriotism as atavistic, a concomitant belief in cosmopolitanism, self-determination and multiculturalism, an emphasis on rights above duties and the restructuring of society around a discourse of equality and human rights.

For Christians in the West, feelings of marginalisation by a culture of secular liberalism have perhaps been even more pronounced. Across a whole range of issues there seems to be an increasingly large and seemingly intractable divide between the ethical discourse of Christian groups and the largely secular voice of the media and policymakers. This is not to say that all Christians agree on these matters, but what is significant is that the common ground by which a debate might be conducted between secular liberals and religious groups seems to be diminishing.

In the first half of the twentieth century, there may have been some debate as to what actually constituted Christian values, but there was no question that the majority of public debate was conducted by reference to Judeo-Christian ethics. In the twenty-first century, secular ideas of human rights and equality are increasingly the dominant ideas by which we are reshaping our society. In this book I will argue that this has created a serious problem for the modern world. The liberal tradition has failed to understand or to take seriously the very human desires for patriotism, kinship and community felt by non-religious citizens, as well as failing to engage with the motivations of religious citizens. As a result, there is an emerging division of moral values within the nation between metropolitan liberals and traditional communities. Yet, interestingly, this is not the first time that the liberal tradition has made this mistake. By retracing the history of liberalism, we can gain an insight into the historical problems it has encountered and what we might expect in our society if such issues continue unaddressed.

Rather than simply offering a critique of liberalism, I will advocate a different approach to politics. In reaction to the cosmopolitanism and multiculturalism of the modern liberal state, far right groups have sought to capitalise upon people's very real desire for a shared identity and community. Many politicians and public figures have expressed a concern at indications of racism and a turning to divisive nationalism. Moving from the idealism of the liberal tradition to a self-serving nationalism would be both dangerous and unwelcome. Throughout this book I shall argue that the conservative tradition provides a genuine alternative to toxic ideologies such as communism and fascism. It is a tradition which has the potential to address the legitimate grievances of those who have been disenfranchised on both the left and the right, while engaging them in a healthy form of politics which resists the desire for sectarian violence and hatred.

The father of conservatism, Edmund Burke, asserted the value of a deeply human approach to politics. He emphasised many of the things which the politically disenfranchised of today feel are lacking: common sense, tradition, patriotism and local loyalties. But importantly he made the claim that such instincts are given to us by God and, in and of themselves, they should define not just our approach to politics, but also the need for these to be located within a grander moral vision.

Burke presents us with an alternative account of the state, a theological account which views God as the founder and sustainer of society. He offers a defence of Britain's Christian heritage against the prospect of what he termed an 'Atheism by Establishment'.[1] He believed such atheism by establishment to be a product of the liberal tradition as he encountered it in his own era. He also offers a defence of the deeply human desires for identity that so many today are looking for. But

---

[1] Edmund Burke, 'Letters on a Regicide Peace', *The Works of The Right Honourable Edmund Burke,* sixteen volumes (London: C. and J. Rivington, 1826-27) Vol. XIII, p. 170.

importantly he identifies these desires as a part of God's creation. We will see how a Christian moral vision reminds us not only of the importance of such desires, but of their moral limits.

My aims in this book then are threefold. First, to examine Edmund Burke's political thought, emphasising its theological character. Secondly, to weigh Burke's approach against that of the liberal tradition. Thirdly, in the light of this analysis, to offer a defence of the application of Burke's thought to politics today.

What is political liberalism?

The influence of what is called 'political liberalism' has received a substantial amount of critical attention, not least from philosophers and theologians. Alasdair MacIntyre's *After Virtue* and *Whose Justice, Which Rationality?* offered a critique of an absolute belief in human reason to act as an impartial arbitrator in public affairs.[2] Stanley Hauerwas, influenced by John Howard Yoder, has argued that the liberal state idolises autonomy by promoting the belief that we have no story except that which we choose.[3] Public figures such as Bishop Michael Nazir-Ali and Peter Hitchens have voiced concerns that, in assuming that religions ought to be privatized, secular liberalism has silenced Christianity in the public sphere and opened the door to more malign ideologies.[4] Former Archbishop George Carey, Peter Hitchens and Bishop Michael have all detected a forgetting of Britain's Christian heritage. They argue that it has been displaced by a strident secular liberalism which arbitrates upon judicial, political and social questions according to a rule of equality and right. Such commentators fear that, despite professing to operate only according to what is neutral and reasonable, the liberal state actually has an agenda which emerges from its view of humankind and society.

[2] Alasdair MacIntyre, *Whose Justice? Which Rationality?* (London: Gerald Duckworth & Co., 1988).

[3] Stanley Hauerwas, *After Christendom* (Nashville, TN: Abingdon Press, 2nd Ed. 1999); *Resident Aliens: Life in the Christian Colony* (Nashville TN, Abingdon Press, 1989).

[4] Peter Hitchens, *The Rage Against God: Why Faith is the Foundation of Civilisation* (London: Continuum, 2010); Michael Nazir-Ali, *Triple Jeopardy for the West* (London: Bloomsbury, 2012); Nazir-Ali, *Triple Jeopardy*, op. cit., Ch. 13.

To attempt a critique of 'liberalism' seems a broad and perhaps even a confused task. As Robert Song points out, 'Perhaps to talk of liberalism (in the singular) rather than liberalisms (in the plural) is to have been deceived into deducing an identity of object from an identity of name.'[5] For this reason I do not seek to offer a straightforward critique of 'liberalism'. I reflect upon a very specific aspect of liberal political history, that is, the contractarian tradition of liberalism. I shall look in detail at its origins, arguing that the defining characteristic of the tradition is a belief that society should be ordered according to an understanding of man as a free, equal and autonomous person.

What is conservatism?

To speak of conservatism is perhaps no less ambiguous. In this book we will look at a stream of conservatism which finds its roots in the thought of Edmund Burke and can be traced through a long line of thinkers from Lord Liverpool and Samuel Coleridge to Lord Salisbury and T.S. Eliot. It is characterised by an awareness of man's fallen nature, a belief in the importance of inherited wisdom and aged institutions and an insistence on the necessity of duty and natural affections. Most importantly it is an approach to politics rooted in the Christian faith.

[5] Robert Song, *Christianity and Liberal Society* (Oxford: Oxford University Press, 2006), p. 9.

Chapter One

Edmund Burke and The Christian Tradition

Edmund Burke was an Irish statesman whose life spanned most of the eighteenth century. He entered Parliament in 1765 and his thought has made an enduring impression on British politics. He is widely seen as the father of conservatism and is famous for being suspicious of abstraction in politics, favouring instead the incremental evolution of institutions. Burke's *magnum opus* was his *Reflections on the Revolution in France,* his response to the prevailing intellectual winds that were blowing across Europe. Burke's *Reflections* were published at an early stage of the French Revolution at which point many Whigs, including Richard Sheridan and Charles James Fox, welcomed the revolution as the dawning of liberty in France, going so far as to call it 'the greatest event it is that ever happened in the world!'.[1] Burke is also known for his defence of the American colonists in their fight against taxation without representation and for his condemnation of Warren Hastings and the despotic actions of the East India Company. One of the reasons that Burke's writings have exercised so much influence upon subsequent generations is because, read in retrospect, they exhibit a remarkable prescience.

Burke's political thought is characterised by his emphasis on historical precedent, his veneration of ancestral and customary wisdom and his condemnation of power unrestrained by law. He is also known for his suspicion of political abstraction, such as the French revolutionaries' 'rights of man'. What is perhaps less clear in contemporary works on Edmund Burke is how a set of Christian theological beliefs exercised a

---

[1] L. G. Mitchell, 'Fox, Charles James (1749–1806)', *Oxford Dictionary of National Biography*, Oxford University Press, 2004; online edition, Oct 2007, http://www. oxforddnb.com/view/article/10024, (accessed 29th April 2013).

substantial influence upon and underpinned his political thought. In this chapter we will look at some of these beliefs.

Burke and the natural law

An important historical point of difference between liberalism and conservatism hinges upon their understanding of human nature. Christian thinkers as early as Saint Paul argued that human beings are fallen and sinful. Yet the Christian tradition has also maintained the belief that God is the author of a moral law that governs his creation and is accessible to humans in spite of our fallen nature. This tradition of ethical thought developed through the centuries and played an important role in European political theory. Perhaps the most significant thinker in the natural law tradition is Saint Thomas Aquinas. Writing in the thirteenth century, Aquinas argued that all creatures (as well as the creation more broadly) are directed towards natural ends ordained by the creator.[2] For Aquinas, human nature, as God created it, naturally seeks the good. Importantly, human beings have an innate ability to judge the right course of action and this can be acted on according to conscience. Yet, to the extent that man is both spiritually fallen and limited in his knowledge, he can only partially attain a true knowledge of the created order.

This tradition of Christian natural law thinking had a significant impact on the English common law tradition and more broadly on political theory in premodern Europe. As a result, in the common law, we find a clearly articulated tradition which precedes Burke in arguing for conservation and the preservation of custom. These are taken to be established by reason and tested by time, and therefore will conform to the natural law. Indeed, the leading lights of the common law tradition clearly and consistently link the law of England, established by custom and precedent, to the natural law. John Fortescue, in his *On the Nature of the Law of Nature*, offers a clear exposition of the natural law as it was understood by Thomas Aquinas. Similarly, other prominent common lawyers, such as Thomas de Littleton, Thomas More, John Selden, Edward Coke and Christopher St. Germain, all reference the natural law and demonstrate a belief that it shaped the laws of England.

---

[2] Thomas Aquinas, *Summa Theologica: Prima Secundae Partis*, trans. Fathers of the English Dominican Province in: *Christian Classics* (Notre Dame, 1981). Q. 90, A. 1.

When we look at the leading thinkers in the tradition, with whom Burke was familiar, we see that they believed the natural law to be critical in informing healthy laws and customs. For these thinkers, the immemorial law of the land is conceptually conjoined to what is essentially a Thomistic understanding of the natural law.

The point is put well by Richard O'Sullivan:

the law of nature was throughout the creative centuries of the common law a familiar idea and a guiding principle among lawyers and judges, and that it may even be said to be the source and spring of the common law as it was conceived and developed by Bracton and Fortescue and Littleton, and Thomas More and Christopher St. Germain, and Coke and Holt, and even by Blackstone.[3]

Thomas Aquinas' influence was not simply restricted to medieval English legal understanding of the natural law but rather we see that, through lawyers such as Fortescue, Selden and Germain, a broadly Thomistic vision of man and society was incorporated into the basic presuppositions of the common law tradition which passed into the eighteenth century. By virtue of the tradition's high esteem for precedent, the assumptions of earlier lawyers exercised a tremendous influence upon their successors.

In the English common law tradition Burke found a rich heritage of medieval Christian writings on natural law which were consistently related to political and legal issues. It was this common law tradition more than any other that informed Burke's political opinions and provided him with a chronicle of the nation's character.

Not only was Burke steeped in the common law, but he was deeply interested in its sources. Indeed, he considered himself sufficiently expert in the origins of the laws of England that in 1757 he embarked upon an essay on the history of the laws of England as part of his *Abridgement of English History*. In this incomplete project, Burke demonstrated an extensive knowledge of the sources of the common law and he was aware of the influence of continental canon law upon the development of the

---

[3] Richard O'Sullivan, K. C., 'Natural Law and Common Law', *Transactions of the Grotius Society,* Vol. 31, (1945), pp. 117-138 and particularly p. 119.

English common law. In 'An Essay Towards an History of the Laws of England', Burke lists 'three capital sources' of the 'Saxon laws' noting 'The second source' was 'the canons of the church', writing that they 'influenced considerably a people, over whom that order had an almost unbounded authority'.[4]

This tradition of natural law informed much of Burke's critique of the French revolutionaries as well as his other writing and speeches. In 1788 Burke wrote: 'We are all born in subjection – all born equally, high and low, governors and governed, in subjection to one great, immutable, pre-existent law' which is 'antecedent to our very existence'. For Burke, it is by this law that 'we are knit and connected in the eternal frame of the universe, out of which we cannot stir.'[5] There is even a case to be made that the natural law is the basis of all the constituent components of his political thought.[6]

Burke and the Anglican Divines

It is also worth drawing attention to the more explicitly theological sources from which Burke's education in the natural law were advanced. In 1780 Burke wrote that he had 'turned his attention to the reading of all the theological publications, on all sides, that were written with such wonderful ability in the last and present century'.[7] Burke possessed an extensive list of theological works in his personal library. St. Augustine, William Chillingworth, Archbishop Leighton, John Tillotson, William Warburton, William Wolaston and James Foster are but a few prominent names.[8] Furthermore, there are references in Burke's writings and speeches to Richard Hooker, Edward Stillingfleet, Joseph Butler, John Leland and Anthony Ellys. If Burke is taken at his word, it seems highly likely that he was familiar with these authors and gave significant weight

[4] Edmund Burke, 'An Essay Towards an History of the Laws of England' in *The Works of Edmund Burke*, Vol. V (Boston, Charles C. Little & James Brown, 1839), p. 726.
[5] Burke, 'Speech in the Impeachment of Warren Hastings', ibid., pp. 165-67.
[6] The most comprehensive work on this topic is Peter Stanlis, *Edmund Burke and the Natural Law* (Lafayette: Huntington House, 1986).
[7] Edmund Burke, 6 June 1780, *Parliamentary History*, 21: 710. Quoted in Francis Canavan, *Edmund Burke: Prescription and Providence* (Durham, NC: Carolina Academic Press, 1987), p. 6.
[8] See *Catalogue of the Library of the Late Right Hon. Edmund Burke* (Oxford: Bodleian Library).

to the importance of their theology. Burke was certainly aware of the distinction between the traditional natural law and the natural rights claimed by the revolutionaries.[9]

Burke, like the common lawyers before him, expressed the belief that the British state had emerged in accordance with the natural law, and he saw the hand of providence actively ordering the state. The state was in some sense sanctified by virtue of its congruence with the natural law. He tells us that 'This great law does not arise from our conventions or compacts; on the contrary, it gives to our conventions and compacts all the force and sanction they can have.' Nor, in his view, does it arise from 'our vain institutions'. But rather, 'Every good gift is of God; all power is of God; and He who has given the power, and from Whom alone it originates, will never suffer the exercise of it to be practised upon any less solid foundation than the power itself.' For Burke, the logical corollary was clear: 'If, then, all dominion of man over man is the effect of the Divine disposition, it is bound by the eternal laws of Him that give it, with which no human authority can dispense.'[10]

In his *Reflections on the Revolution in France*, Burke draws heavily upon the natural law in his criticisms of the French revolutionaries. Burke articulates a teleological account of both man and the state, which is to say that he saw them as created by God for specific ends. He is clear that God is both the 'author and protector of civil society', and that God willed civil society because without it, 'man could not by any possibility arrive at the perfection of which his nature is capable, nor even make a remote and faint approach to it.' It was for these ends that God willed the state and 'willed its connection with the source and original archetype of all perfection.'[11]

---

[9] This point has been missed by some critics of the natural law school, for instance see Drew Maciag, *Edmund Burke in America: The Contested Career of the Father of Modern Conservatism* (Ithaca, NY: Cornell University Press, 2013). In this work, the author seems to conflate natural law and natural right and in doing so comes to the conclusion that Burke made contradictory statements on the topic. Leo Strauss argues convincingly that Burke looked back to a premodern tradition in the face of natural rights theorists. See Leo Strauss, *Natural Right and History* (Chicago IL: University of Chicago Press, 1963).

[10] Burke, 'Speech in the Impeachment of Warren Hastings', *The Works*, op. cit., Vol. XIII, pp. 166-167.

[11] Burke, *Reflections on the Revolution in France*, *The Works of The Right Honourable Edmund Burke*, sixteen volumes (London: C. and J. Rivington, 1826-27), Vol. V, pp. 185-187.

The Burke scholar Francis Canavan notes the importance of this passage, writing that 'In Burke's philosophy there can be no merely secular society because there is no merely secular world'. Indeed, one of the most remarkable things about this passage is that in a political tract Burke embarks upon an exposition of society which clearly bears the hallmarks of the natural law tradition. This passage implicitly assumes a human teleology which is ordered towards the perfection of the creator; society is conceived as a corporate body, endowed with laws and sovereignty which connect it to God. Society is seen as a means by which man is able to cultivate his own virtue in community with others.

Burke's understanding of the natural law is of a law that is actively engaged throughout history in ordering societies towards their right ends wherever the precepts of the natural law are rightly adhered to in concrete circumstances. The common lawyers' belief in the natural law gives us an insight into why they were so keenly aware of the importance of history and the continuity of society, the chief reason being that the flourishing of right order requires time. Burke feared that a society which revered reason alone would seek to destroy the amassed wisdom which had been accrued over the course of ages. The instinct to conserve then is, at least in part, attuned to a theological belief in the providential ordering of society by God. Burke clearly expresses a belief in such providence, and this belief did not preclude the importance of human agency in the divine plan. On the contrary, Burke believed humans to have a choice as to whether or not they adhere to God's law. In Burke's eyes, revolutionaries, 'appear[ed] rather to resist the decrees of Providence itself, than the mere designs of men.'[12] Burke believed that man had an important role to play in the social order and that, if he was to act rightly, then prudence was an indispensable virtue.

The virtue of prudence

For Burke, prudence was the bridge between the natural moral law and the contingent set of circumstances in which any human society exists. By definition, prudential reasoning possesses a moral dimension and Burke was clear that prudence seeks the good within any particular set of circumstances: 'God forbid that prudence, the first of all virtues, as

---

[12] Burke, 'Thoughts on French Affairs', *The Works*, op. cit., Vol. VII, p. 85.

well as the supreme director of them all, should ever be employed in the service of any of the vices.'[13] For Burke, the role of the prudential statesman was to deliberate upon the moral course of action in particular circumstances without speculating upon utopian schemes to recast society at large. For Burke, prudence was not only 'the first in rank of the virtues political and moral, but she is the director, the regulator, the standard of them all.'[14] Rejecting a faith in abstract human reason alone, prudence was the touchstone to which Burke consistently returned in political questions.

In Burke's writings we see that his commendation of the piecemeal operation of prudence is made, in part, on the basis that human beings are both made in the image of God and fallen. To reason prudentially, men do not need to know God's mind, they do not need to be capable of listing the universal rights of men, nor do they need to be capable of deducing an ideal form of government. Instead, prudence, informed by culture, education and the natural moral law is seen as the guiding light of the statesman. For this reason, Burke was able to view political order as 'a joint product of God and man, in which the order of society – derived from and reflecting the divinely-ordained order of the universe – was produced, maintained and improved by the constant exercise of man's political reason'.[15] It is in this context that man can be a co-creator with God, not seeking to be the architect himself, but following the prudential course in each circumstance.

Burke was aware that the myriad of contingencies which surround a society will inevitably alter their form of government; as he put it, 'People must be governed in a manner agreeable to their temper and disposition'.[16] As we will see, the idealistic political structure of the French revolutionaries had no room for history or considerations of locality. Burke was to perceive with some prescience that precisely because the natural rights discourse of the revolutionaries was ahistorical

[13] Burke, 'Speech in the Impeachment of Warren Hastings', *The Works*, op. cit., Vol. XIII, p. 275.
[14] Burke, 'Appeal from the New to the Old Whigs', *The Works*, op. cit., Vol. XI, p. 98.
[15] Francis Canavan, 'Edmund Burke's Conception of the Role of Reason in Politics' in Iain Hampsher-Monk ed., *Edmund Burke*, (Farnham: Ashgate, 2009) p. 34.
[16] Edmund Burke, 'Observations on a Late State of the Nation', *The Works*, op. cit., Vol. II, p. 166.

and abstract it would strip society of all that was deemed to be superfluous; foremost in the line of fire would be the Christian religion.

Burke and the Christian religion

The abstraction and ahistoricism of the French *philosophes* was not merely academic. Their neglect of the teleology of existing institutions, coupled with a disdain for the French *ancien regime* (though there was much to criticise in this), meant that they regarded the existing institutions as illegitimate. Burke suspected that behind the veneer of liberal discourse the French revolutionaries really desired the 'utter abolition, under any of its forms, of the Christian religion', noting this with some irony given that 'we hear these new teachers continually boasting of their spirit of toleration.'[394] In this suspicion Burke was to be vindicated. Charles A. Gliozzo documents some of the anti-religious activities which characterised the revolution, listing 'aggressive anti-clericalism, prohibition of any Christian practice or worship either in public or private life, closing of the churches, the formation of a revolutionary calendar to replace the Christian one, and the establishment of new religious cults – the Cult of Reason and the Cult of the Supreme Being'.[17] He argues that it was no coincidence that the revolution was so profoundly anti-religious, due to the fact that a 'direct influence can be traced from the *philosophes* to the de-christianizers of the Revolution'.[18]

Voltaire rejected the idea of the Christian God, referring instead to the Supreme Being. He also advocated that all ecclesiastical hierarchy should be destroyed. Similarly Rousseau's notion of spirituality envisaged the lone individual in an idealised state of nature, employing his reason to discover the Supreme Being. Burke was deeply critical of Helvetius, Voltaire, Rousseau 'and the rest of that infamous gang', identifying in their thought a systematic attempt to purge society of religion:

> We cannot be ignorant of the spirit of atheistical fanaticism, inspired by a multitude of writings, dispersed with incredible assiduity and expense, and by sermons delivered in all the streets and places of

---

[17] Charles A. Gliozzo 'The Philosophes and Religion: Intellectual Origins of the Dechristianization Movement in the French Revolution', *Church History*, Vol. 40, No. 3 (Sep., 1971), pp. 273-283 and particularly p. 273.
[18] Ibid.

public resort in Paris. These writings and sermons have filled the populace with a black and savage atrocity of mind, which supersedes in them the common feeling of morality and religion.[19]

Burke believed that they were motivated by their own vanity: 'When your lords had many writers as immoral as the object of their statue (such as Voltaire and others) they chose Rousseau, because in him that peculiar vice [vanity] which they wished to erect into a ruling virtue was by far the most conspicuous.'[20]

Significant intellectual figures such as Voltaire, Rousseau and Helvetius were deeply sceptical of tradition, revelation and inherited wisdom and, in different ways, championed the liberating power of reason. Gliozzo writes that the '*Philosophes*... determined human nature empirically, for they perceived in men not their relationship to an objective world of ends and values, but their actual needs, wants, feelings inclinations and ideas. They taught that by reason, man may be the master of things and of himself, that he can imagine a society in which all men enjoy freedom and happiness, and that he can deliberately create the society he has imagined'.[21]

In the writings of the *philosophes* we see the belief that right political order can be deduced by reason alone. Consequently, the French revolution was animated by a form of political thought that had little interest in traditional religion or inherited wisdom. It is therefore no surprise that the political heirs of the *philosophes* had such contempt for the institutional Church. Gliozzo notes that 'though Voltaire, Rousseau, Diderot, and Helvetius were often in disagreement, they were united in common goals: the movement for a better society and the destruction of traditional Christianity'.[22] Echoing this point, Roger Scruton writes, 'The Revolution involved a war against religion: an attempt to re-create the world as a world uncreated.'[23] This was one of the features of the

---

[19] Burke, *Reflections on the Revolution in France*, op. cit., p. 278.
[20] Burke, 'Letter to a Member of the National Assembly', *The Works*, op. cit., Vol VI, p. 32.
[21] Gliozzo, op cit., p. 283.
[22] Ibid.
[23] Roger Scruton, 'Man's Second Disobedience: a Vindication of Burke' in Iain Hampsher-Monk (ed.), *Edmund Burke*, (Farnham: Ashgate, 2009), p. 430.

revolution which Burke found most disturbing.

We shall see that most of the revolutionaries were atheists, deists and dissenters, a fact of which Burke was well aware. Burke clearly saw a direct link between the theological beliefs of the rationalist dissenters and the political ideas which he found to be most troubling – whether it was in their rejection of the natural affections, the optimistic view of man in the state of nature, the profession of natural rights, their rejection of tradition or their overt attacks upon Christianity. All of these political ideas were derived primarily from atheistic and deistic beliefs. In this respect, we can almost tell as much about Burke's theological beliefs by looking at the political ideas that he attacked as we can by analysing those he defended.

Burke affirmed a distinct religious tradition in Britain which, he argued, had been at work in the country's national character for centuries. He states 'We are Protestants, not from indifference but from zeal.'[24] Burke speaks of the 'Christian religion which has hitherto been our boast and comfort', insisting that whilst we do not 'Violently condemn... the Greek nor the Armenian, nor, since heats are subsided, the Roman system of religion, we prefer the Protestant, not because we think it has less of the Christian religion in it, but because, in our judgment, it has more'. For Burke, the religion which helped to form a particular society was deeply important to that society's institutions and values. Moreover, Burke was zealous for the cause of Christianity in Britain because he believed it to be true.

Burke writes, 'religion is the basis of civil society and the source of all good and of all comfort'.[25] For Burke, the civil is intimately involved in the formation of the political, and the two occupy overlapping jurisdictions. Ian Harris points out that for Burke 'Christianity generated benefits not only to the individual's soul... but also to political arrangements'.[26] Interestingly, Burke does not preclude non-Christian religions from being a social asset, writing that 'where the Hindoo

---

[24] Burke, *Reflections on the Revolution in France*, op. cit., p. 174.
[25] Burke, *Reflections on the Revolution in France*, op. cit., p. 173.
[26] Ian Harris 'Burke and Religion' in Christopher Insole and David Dwan, (eds.), *The Cambridge Companion to Edmund Burke* (Cambridge: Cambridge University Press, 2012), p. 135.

religion has been established, that country has been flourishing'.[27] Harris notes that statements such as these did not imply any sort of relativism for Burke, who was committed to the truth of Christianity; rather, Burke is observing the social utility of religious traditions. Yet Harris makes one further point; he states that 'the religion which has become bound up with a society is the one that suits it'. Therefore an assault upon the established religion of a society is 'likely to produce retrogression' in that state.[28] This point is well illustrated in Burke's discussion of the history of India, as he writes of 'the time of the prophet Mahomed' in which 'that proud and domineering sect' used 'the ferocious arm of their prophetic sword to change the religion and manners of that country' to dire effect.[29]

The fact that Christianity had been such an important influence upon the political formation of both Britain and France was important to Burke. He followed Hooker in conceiving the Church and state as an organic whole. He writes: 'In a Christian commonwealth the Church and the State are one and the same thing; being different integrant parts of the same whole'.[30] This is perhaps never clearer than in the *Reflections*. Burke writes that 'all the good things which are connected with manner and civilization' have 'depended upon two principles... the spirit of a gentleman and the spirit of religion'.[31] Burke believed that 'religion is the basis of civil society' because, in his view, 'man is by his constitution a religious animal'.[32] He argued that religion ought to bear upon every area of an individual's life and he was deeply suspicious of any attempt to extricate religion from society. He writes that 'If our religious tenets should ever want a further elucidation, we shall not call on atheism to explain them. We shall not light up our temple from that unhallowed fire.'[33] In his belief that society was inextricably linked to the religious and civil institutions which compose it, he writes that 'instead of quarrelling with establishments, as some do who have made

---

[27] Burke, 'Speech in the Impeachment of Warren Hastings', *The Works*, op. cit., p. 72.
[28] Harris, op. cit., p. 138.
[29] Burke, 'Speech in the Impeachment of Warren Hastings', *The Works*, op. cit., pp. 75-76.
[30] Burke quoted in Harris, op cit., p. 137.
[31] Burke, *Reflections on the Revolution in France*, op. cit., p. 154.
[32] Ibid., p. 174.
[33] Ibid., p. 173.

a philosophy and a religion of their hostility to such institutions, we cleave closely to them'.[34]

In this Burke was articulating the conviction of the vast majority of Whigs and Tories, whether or not they hoped for the further political emancipation of dissenters and Catholics. By one estimate, in 1760 over 92 per cent of the nation professed a belief in the established Anglican faith. There were almost no self-confessed atheists and only around one percent of the nation were Catholics, whilst the total number of dissenters, non-conformists and Jews did not account for more than five per cent of the nation.[35] This gives us an insight into quite how radical the thought of the French *Philosophes* was to a British audience. Burke, like most of his countrymen, envisaged Christianity as the very basis of British and French society, because both societies had been formed out of Christian belief.

In the first of his *Letters on a Regicide Peace*, Burke wrote that 'The whole of the polity and economy of every country in Europe has been derived from the same sources', chiefly 'the very same Christian religion'.[36] Similarly, in Burke's *Abridgement of English History*, which he began composing as early as 1757, the benign effect of Christianity upon the customs of the English people is made clear. He relates how, after reunifying the kingdoms of England, Alfred found 'the whole face of things in the most desperate condition: there was no observance of law and order; religion had no force; there was no honest industry; the most squalid poverty and the grossest ignorance had overspread the whole kingdom.' He then tells us that Alfred resolved to revive and improve the Saxon institutions:

> The Christian religion, having once taken root in Kent, spread itself with great rapidity throughout all the other Saxon kingdoms in England. The manners of the Saxons underwent a notable alteration by this change in their religion: their ferocity was much abated; they became more mild and sociable; and their laws began to partake of

---

[34] Ibid., p. 175.
[35] Clive Field, 'Counting Religion in England and Wales: The Long Eighteenth Century, c. 1680 - c.1840', *Journal of Ecclesiastical History*, Vol. 63., No. 4, October 2012, pp. 693-720.
[36] Burke, 'Letters on a Regicide Peace', *The Works*, op. cit., Vol. XIII, p. 181.

the softness of their manners, everywhere recommending mercy and a tenderness for Christian blood. There never was any people who embraced religion with a more fervent zeal than the Anglo Saxons, nor with more simplicity of spirit.[37]

It was not simply religion, but the Christian message in particular, which Burke believed had a socially benign effect on a people.

Burke and the Church

Burke was clear regarding the social benefits of religion, and of Christianity, but what of the institutional Church itself? The Burke scholar Conor Cruise O'Brien has argued that Burke's Anglicanism was a matter of expediency and that, in reality, his sympathies remained with the Catholicism of his homeland.[38] It is true that Burke did petition for dissenters and despised the oppression of Catholics in Ireland, as is made clear in his unpublished *Tract Relative to the Laws against Popery*. Yet, in spite of this, there is little evidence that he was anything other than a committed Anglican establishmentarian throughout his life. As early as 1765 he wrote to Rockingham to assure him that he was not a Catholic; understandably, given his Irish background, Catholicism was an issue about which Burke was deeply sensitive. For example, in 1770 he chastised his dear friend Richard Shackleton for having given information to an English enquirer regarding the religious background of his mother and wife; Burke was less than impressed that the information had found its way into the *London Evening Post*. In 1772 Burke gave his *Speech on the Acts of Uniformity* arguing against the liberalisation of the clergy's subscription to the thirty-nine articles. In this speech, he shows himself to be a fierce defender of Church establishment, arguing that the Union of 1707 would be endangered should the clergy's subscription be relaxed.

Similarly, Burke spoke passionately in the House of Commons in 1790 on a Bill for the repeal of the Test and Corporation Acts which

---

[37] Burke, 'An Abridgement of English History: from the Invasion of Julius Caesar to the end of the Reign of King John', *The Works*, op. cit., Vol. X, p. 282.

[38] See, Conor Cruise O'Brien, *The Great Melody: A Thematic Biography of Edmund Burke* (Chicago: University of Chicago Press, 1994).

required the holders of military and civil offices to be communicants of the Church of England. In his speech, Burke connected rationalist dissenters to the subversion of the Church and the state, arguing that 'the leading preachers among the dissenters were avowed enemies to the Church of England'.[39] He cited two catechisms produced by a Mr. Robinson and a Mr. Palmer, his central concern being that the first catechism 'contained no precept of religion whatsoever'. He proceeded to argue that 'The catechisms were filled with invective against kings and bishops, in which everything was misrepresented'.[40] He quoted from the rationalist dissenters Joseph Priestley and Richard Price in order to show that leading dissenters were intent on the disestablishment and destruction of the Church.

Rejecting the arguments of revolutionaries, Burke held that instead of having 'abstract principles of natural right', Britain had 'what was much better, society, which substituted wisdom and justice, in the room of original right', proceeding to say that society 'took in all the virtue of the virtuous, all the wisdom of the wise. It gave life, security, and action to every faculty of the soul, and secured the possession of every comfort which those proud and boasting natural rights impotently held out.'

The most interesting aspect of this speech is the role that Burke gives to the Church in his argument. After listing the virtues of society, he writes: 'Such were the advantages attributable to society, and also deducible from the church, which was the necessary creature and assistant of society in all its great and most beneficial purposes.' He professes a 'peculiar regard and reverence for the established church' and speaks of the necessity 'to preserve it safe and entire at a time like the present'.[41] Equally, Burke cautions against Protestant fervour that could destabilise the state, as it nearly did in the Gordon Riots of 1780.[42] However, it is perhaps in the *Reflections on the French Revolution* that we hear Burke at his most passionate in defending the established Church.

The treatment of the French Church at the hands of the revolutionaries

---

[39] Edmund Burke, 'Speech on Repeal of the Test and Corporation Acts' (1790) in *The Speeches of the Right Honourable Edmund Burke in the House of Commons and in Westminster Hall in Four Volumes*, Vol. III, (London: A. Strahan, 1816), p. 480.

[40] Ibid., p. 477.

[41] Ibid., p. 476.

[42] See ibid., pp. 473-483.

horrified Burke and he feared that the Church of England could suffer a similar fate. We will see that liberals such as John Locke argued that there was an unassailable divide between the functions of Church and state. The dominant wing of the French revolutionaries took this idea to a new level and, instead of the state supporting the church, they sought to delegitimize it.[43] As one commentator puts it, 'Nobody had ever expected that, once the reform of France began, the Church would remain untouched.'[44] The revolutionaries articulated a clear link between the elevation of reason and the denigration of religion, seeing it as a threat to man's authority.

In theory, the authors of the revolutionary *Declaration of the Rights of Man and of the Citizen* had established a freedom of equality, freedom of expression, freedom to run for public office and the extension of equal civil rights; yet some proved to be more equal than others. As early as 1789 'Clerical speakers were regularly jeered in the gallery', 'all monasteries and convents, except those dedicated to educational and charitable work, were dissolved, and new religious vows were forbidden.'[45] By 1790, still an early stage in the French revolution, it was increasingly clear that freedom of conscience was to be severely circumscribed. On 27th November the deputies resolved to 'dismiss at once all clerics who did not accept the new order unequivocally. And to test this acceptance they imposed an oath. All beneficed clergy were to swear after mass on the first available Sunday 'to be faithful to the nation, the king and the law, and to uphold with all their power the constitution declared by the National Assembly and accepted by the king.'[46] At this stage the Pope involved himself in the dispute, composing a letter of objection; 'In Paris, the pope was burned in effigy and hostile crowds prevented refractory priests and their congregations from exercising the freedom of worship vouchsafed as one of the Rights of Man and the Citizen.'[47] Worse was to follow as the Revolution unfolded.

[43] Israel Jonathan I. *Revolutionary Ideas: An Intellectual History of the French Revolution from The Rights of Man to Robespierre* (Princeton, NJ: Princeton University Press, 2014).
[44] Doyle, William, *Oxford History of the French Revolution*, (Oxford: Oxford University Press, 2nd edition, 2002), p. 136.
[45] Ibid., p. 137.
[46] Ibid., p. 144.
[47] Ibid., p. 146.

Burke's *Reflections* is marked by the conviction that the established Christian religion is integral to the social and political order of the nation. Burke writes that 'We are resolved to keep an established church, an established monarchy, an established aristocracy, and an established democracy, each in the degree it exists, and in no greater.'[48] He believed a direct corollary of 'the destruction of the Christian religion' was 'a persecution which would strike at property, liberty and life'.[49] Burke was clear that the Church is a defender of liberty, not an oppressor. He wrote that 'I think that Church harmonises with our civil constitution, with the frame and fashion of our Society, and with the general Temper of the people. I think it is better calculated all circumstances considered, for keeping peace amongst the different sects, and of affording to them a reasonable protection, than any other System.'[50]

However, Burke was keenly aware of the danger of close Church-state relations, writing that 'politics and the pulpit are terms that have little agreement', and stating that, 'The cause of civil liberty and civil government gains as little as that of religion by this confusion of duties.'[51] Is this a contradiction then from his prior statement that 'the church establishment' is not 'convenient' but 'essential' to the state and the 'foundation of [the] whole constitution, with which, and with every part of which, it holds an indissoluble union'? [52] In direct opposition to men like Richard Price, Burke was differentiating between a functional communion of Church and state and the moral communion of Church and state. Burke was rightly wary of allowing the Church to dictate policy on particular political issues, yet this in no way marginalised the importance of the Church in composing the moral fabric of the nation. The Church should undergird society with its moral authority, but Burke was cautioning us against those who wish to determine decisions in politics despite having 'nothing of politics but the passions they excite'.[53] Yet this did not stop him from envisaging a government and judiciary

---

[48] Burke, *Reflections on the Revolution in France*, op. cit., p. 175.

[49] Ibid., p. 209.

[50] Burke, 'Letter from Burke to an unknown person Jan 20, 1791' in M. W. McConnell, 'Establishment and Toleration in Edmund Burke's "Constitution of Freedom"' *The Supreme Court Review* (1995), pp. 393-462.

[51] Burke, *Reflections on the Revolution in France*, op. cit., p. 42.

[52] Ibid., p. 188.

[53] Ibid., p. 48.

which is moulded by a particular theological tradition.

For Burke, the established church ought to inform the moral sensibilities of the people. This infusion of moral teaching extends to legislators, judges, aristocrats as well as the common person. Burke was explicit that the Church should never be relegated from the public sphere into a private enclave: 'with a parental solicitude, we have not relegated religion (like something we were ashamed to show) to obscure municipalities or rustic villages. No! We will have her to exalt her mitred front in courts and parliaments. We will have her mixed throughout the whole mass of life and blended with all the classes of society.'[54] In such passages we can see that he believed the moral instincts of a people ought to be informed by the Christian faith through the medium of the institutional church. In this picture, being a Christian nation is not simply about adhering to a specific set of doctrines or having an institutional church; it is about cultivating a shared moral vision and a character which is informed by the moral content of the Christian religion.[55]

In their belief that reason could arrive at a formula for the perfect society, the revolutionaries were attempting to circumvent the mediating role of time and prudence. Burke predicted that, as a result, the revolutionaries would despise the Church, whose traditions and deferral to revelation epitomised that which the Jacobins loathed. In attacking the Church, Burke believed that the revolutionaries were disembowelling the moral core of the nation. Given the course which the revolution subsequently took, it is hard to avoid the conclusion that Burke's concerns were legitimate.

Burke on God and Social Order

For Burke, society was both a contract between the living and the dead, and a contract between man and God. God's mystical action is present in society from its conception onwards; God is envisaged as the very 'founder of society'. For Burke, this meant that the constitution was in some sense sanctified. This belief impacted Burke's view of man's

---

[54] Ibid., p. 195.
[55] Such sentiments are also clearly expressed by Hooker. See Richard Hooker, *Of the Laws of Ecclesiastical Polity*, Vol. I, ed. Stephen McGrade (Oxford University Press, 2013).

relationship to society. For Burke, men and women are born into a society with obligations and fraternal bonds already incumbent upon them. This is man's natural habitat, as opposed to a solitary state of nature.

In his 'Appeal from the New to the Old Whigs', he explains these themes. He tells us the 'author of our being is the author of our place in the order of existence' and that he has positioned us 'not according to our will, but according to his'. Because of this, 'We have obligations to mankind at large, which are not in consequence of any special voluntary pact.' For Burke, man's love for his fellow man should arise simply from 'the relation of man to man, and the relation of man to God'. It is precisely because of these 'prior obligations' that 'the force of all the pacts which we enter into with any particular person or number of persons amongst mankind' exists. By way of example, Burke notes that 'When we marry, the choice is voluntary, but the duties are not matter of choice.'

Burke is emphasising the created order that God has given us, in which duties are as real as our own rights: 'The instincts which give rise to this mysterious process of nature are not of our making. But out of physical causes, unknown to us, perhaps unknowable, arise moral duties, which, as we are able perfectly to comprehend, we are bound indispensably to perform.' He points out that parents have 'never made a convention of any sort' with their children. Likewise, 'Children are not consenting to their relation, but their relation, without their actual consent, binds them to its duties'. These duties arise from the fact that 'every rational creature is in unison with the predisposed order of things.' In short they are ordered by God's natural law.

By the same token, humans have an obligation to their country. We are told that 'without any stipulation, on our part, are we bound by that relation called our country'. Moreover, we are given 'powerful instincts to make this duty as dear and grateful to us, as it is awful and coercive. Our country is not a thing of mere physical locality. It consists, in a great measure, in the ancient order into which we are born. We may have the same geographical situation, but another country; as we may have the same country in another soil. The place that determines our duty to our country is a social, civil relation.'[56]

---

[56] Burke, 'Appeal from the New to the Old Whigs', *The Works*, op. cit., Vol. XI, pp. 206-207.

For Burke, the fraternal bonds which knit society together are not born out of a human contract, nor are they a product of reason, but they are given to us by a divine authority. He also tells us that we are born with divinely ordained obligations which, like the whole 'order of existence', are grounded in God's authority. We can see why, for Burke, any thought experiment which conceives of humans as free, equal and dislocated is unlikely to offer useful conclusions for the real concrete existence of actual humans. We have seen that Burke suspected that the 'reason' which the revolutionaries championed was in fact just an expression of their own human desires, and therefore their own will. For this reason Burke rejected any notion of choosing constitutional essentials and argued that the self is not prior to society and the will of individuals must be subordinate to the wisdom of ages, which accords with the divine moral law and which resides in the constitution and in legal precedent. The *philosophes* espoused the idea that society is not organic and God-given but is a result of a "social contract" between the rulers and their subjects. The basis of political authority is one of the defining differences between the contractarian tradition and Burke's thought. For Burke there were duties on the part of the ruler and the subject to each other and to God. These can be seen in the coronation oaths, such as the one taken by King Edgar when he was crowned at Bath in AD 973. But the source of the obligations was not the autonomous free will of individuals entering into a contract, but a reflection of a pre-existing natural order. Whether it be the spiritual authority of the Church, the legal authority of the constitution, the authority of our natural prejudices or the customary authority of the forefathers, all of these were deeply important anchors for Burke, who took the view that we live in a universe in which legitimately grounded authority precedes human will. Burke's suspicion of unrestrained human will can be encapsulated in his statement: 'Law and arbitrary power are in eternal enmity... he, that will substitute *will* in the place of [law], is an enemy to God'.[57]

---

[57] Burke, 'Speech in the Impeachment of Warren Hastings', *The Works*, op. cit., Vol. IX, p. 169.

Summary

In this chapter we have seen that Burke's understanding of the natural law and its relation to the constitution was heavily influenced by pre-modern Christian thinkers. We have seen that Burke rejected the notion that political reason, operating upon a conception of the rights of man, could bring in a new form of government which would bring an end to injustice. Fearful at the potentially revolutionary consequences of such ideas, we have seen that Burke advocated the operation of prudence in political affairs. As a student of the common law tradition, Burke was aware of the idea that the natural law operating through prudence was the chief source of formation for the British constitution. We saw that Burke's understanding of prudence was both religious and deeply tied to his Christian worldview. Contrary to the ideas of the French revolutionaries, we have seen that Burke held the view that the Church was an integral part of the state which unified the nation and provided the people with a moral orientation. We have seen that Burke rejected the notion of a secular society, believing that it was a Christian society which provided the surest possibility for civil concord.

Now that we have looked in some detail at the political thought of Edmund Burke and the theological beliefs that underpinned his thought, we will look in more detail at the tradition that Burke was fighting against. While Burke's struggle was with the revolutionaries, the roots of contractarian liberalism go back a century further. To properly understand liberalism today, we must look to the great English philosopher, John Locke.

Chapter Two

John Locke and the Roots of Political Liberalism

Born amidst the throes of the English Civil War, John Locke was raised in a nation charged with religious and political tensions. Only seventeen years of age when Charles I was executed by Parliamentarians, it seems likely that such political tumult would have left an indelible impression upon the young Locke, especially given that his father was a member of Cromwell's army. Locke completed his time at Westminster school and in 1652 proceeded to study at Christ Church, Oxford. Locke declined the opportunity to take holy orders, choosing to study medicine instead.[1] Significantly, Locke's earliest writings were of an absolutist tone. In political tracts he argued that there was no room for toleration towards those who dissent from the magistrate, even if they did so out of religious loyalties, and this lack of toleration even extended to *adiaphora* (matters of doctrine that were not considered fundamental).[2] His early work displays an uncompromising doctrine of civil obedience. As we shall see, there is an evident shift between this younger Locke and the Locke who penned *A Letter Concerning Toleration* in the 1680s.

In 1667 Locke went to London to live with Anthony Ashley Cooper, the man who would later become the Earl of Shaftesbury. Through his acquaintance with Shaftesbury Locke became involved in the colonial and political issues of his day, acting as an adviser to one of the most

[1] Richard Ashcraft, *Locke's Two Treatises of Government* (Abingdon: Routledge, 2010), pp. 13-14.
[2] See Ingrid Crepell, *Toleration and Identity: Foundations in Early Modern Thought* (Abingdon: Routledge, 2003), p. 97.

prominent political voices in the country.[3] Throughout the 1670s, under the influence of Shaftesbury, Locke became increasingly critical of the establishment, overseen by Charles II. In 1675 a pamphlet entitled 'A Letter from a Person of Quality to His Friend in the Country' appeared, criticising the established ecclesial and political hierarchy and warning of its absolutist aspirations.[4] Whilst it is impossible to know for sure, it has always been suspected that Locke played a hand in its composition. It is notable that Locke left for France soon after the dissemination of the letter and did not return to England until 1678. In 1683, during a period in which Locke was embroiled in the issue of toleration, he again left England, temporarily residing in the Netherlands after being implicated in The Rye House Plot, a failed attempt to assassinate Charles II. In 1685 Charles II's illegitimate son Lord Monmouth invaded England in an unsuccessful attempt to depose his Catholic uncle James II. It was only in 1688, after the Glorious Revolution which installed William of Orange and James II's daughter Mary as monarchs and deposed the Catholic James II that Locke was able to return to his native soil. It was in the aftermath of these great political and religious turbulences that Locke published his *Letter Concerning Toleration* (1689) and his *Two Treatises of Government* (1689).[5] Locke was addressing a society, and indeed a continent, which had endured a century of sectarian strife and was still in the throes of political unrest.

Deductive thought in the seventeenth century

Before looking at Locke's work, it is important to note the intellectual context in which it was written. From late 1619 René Descartes conceived a grand system of thought which extended to medicine, ethics and politics, operating by a method analogous to mathematical reasoning. His system was to be *a priori* and drawn from axiomatic first

---

[3] Ashcraft, *Locke's Two Treatises*, op. cit., p. 21. It is worth noting the colonial context of Locke, which has been emphasised in an essay by David Armitage, who argues that Locke's involvement in the affairs of the Carolina colonies during the early 1670s was particularly significant in the formation of Locke's concept of property rights and political liberalism. See David Armitage, 'John Locke, Carolina and the Two Treatises of Government', *Political Theory*, Vol. 32, No. 5 (2004), pp. 602-627.

[4] See Ashcraft, op. cit., p. 67.

[5] These were likely written between 1679-1680. See Peter Laslett, *Two Treatises of Government*, (Cambridge: Cambridge University Press, 1988).

principles.[6] In England, Thomas Hobbes had embarked upon a similar project. Repeatedly in *Leviathan* (1651) we are told that it is possible to arrive at infallible ethical and political knowledge by means of the same methods which had proved so efficacious in physics.

In *De Cive* Hobbes informs us that if we can render 'the nature of humane Actions as distinctly knowne, as the nature of Quantity in Geometricall Figures... Mankinde should enjoy such an Immortall peace, that... there would hardly be left any pretence for war'.[7] As one commentator points out, 'When ethics and politics are developed by a similar deductive method the whole system necessarily depends on the selection of first principles.'[8] As a materialist, Hobbes made motion subject to mathematical laws the bedrock of his philosophy. He believed that, since men were subject to these same laws, all that was needed was a sufficient knowledge of mankind's appetites and passions and that from this we could extrapolate (in a manner analogous to geometry) an ideal model for society.[9]

Hobbes was far from alone in his faith in the power of deductive reasoning, given the correct first principles. The belief that ethics was a distinct branch of scientific enquiry capable of deductive demonstration was advocated by Leibniz, Spinoza and indeed John Locke.

How then does this relate to modern liberalism? The answer lies in *why* the early liberals hoped to demonstrate that politics and ethics were capable of mathematical demonstration. It is no coincidence that, following an era in which large parts of Europe had struggled to achieve civil concord between religious parties who dogmatically maintained opposing beliefs, pure reason became a wellspring of hope to war-weary Europeans. The result was a quest for a form of government which could stand on principles that were clear to all reasonable men, as opposed to

[6] See René Descartes, *The Method, Meditations, and Selections from the Principles,* trans. John Veitch, (Edinburgh, W. Blackwood & Sons, 6th Ed., 1879), p. 184. See also Louis I. Bredvold, 'The Invention of the Ethical Calculus' in Richard Foster Jones (ed.), *The Seventeenth Century* (Stanford, CA: Stanford University Press, 1951) pp. 165-66. Descartes contemporary Galileo articulates similar themes in *The Assayer* (1623).

[7] Thomas Hobbes, *De Cive*, (London: J.C. for R. Royston, 1651), p. 150.

[8] Bredvold, op. cit., p. 169.

[9] See Thomas Hobbes, *Leviathan*, ed. Richard Tuck (Cambridge University Press, 1991).

the claims of religious faith. As we will see, this aversion to metaphysical claims became a secularising trend that has become more pronounced as the liberal tradition has developed. The liberal tradition presents its founding truths as self-evident facts, not articles of faith. The most important of these self-evident truths is the belief that all men are free and autonomous, endowed with natural rights.

The Natural Law and Natural Rights

An important result of this quest for demonstrable moral reason was a shift in the presentation of the natural law. Premodern natural law was a law which was seen to actively direct creatures towards the natural ends ordained by their creator, impacting their reason, appetites, desires and consciences. In the early modern period natural law came to be construed simply as the capacity of human reason to identify fundamental ideas in nature. We shall see that the natural law is understood in Locke's *Second Treatise* as the capacity of human reason to identify anthropological facts in the state of nature. This helped to make its claims more palatable, and ostensibly objective, to both sceptics and religious absolutists.

Richard Tuck argues that the transition between scholastic and modern understandings of the natural law theories was rooted in scepticism and reactions to it. In his view:

> Grotius and his successors were responding to a straightforward pre-Humean moral scepticism, which simply pointed to the multiplicity of beliefs and practices around the world, and concluded that there were no common moral beliefs and hence nothing stable upon which to build a universal ethics. Part of their response consisted equally simply in demonstrating that there were actually at least two universal moral beliefs (the right of self-preservation and the ban on wanton injury).

Such thinkers concluded that 'this minimalist ethics could be used as a basis for a universal moral science. There was therefore a substantial element of descriptive ethical sociology in their works, since that was the battleground chosen by their opponents.'[10] Tuck concludes that in the period we see a 'continued attempt to integrate the laws of nature into a system based on the principle of self- preservation'.[11] The relevance of all of this to modern liberalism will become clear, but the key point is that in order to placate the sceptics (and religious groups who could not agree), Locke was trying to arrive at a moral fact that all parties could agree on. In doing so, Locke planted the intellectual seed for a society whose foundational belief was not the created moral order of the Christian faith but the idea of an autonomous human endowed with natural rights.[12]

Unlike Thomas Aquinas, who believed that 'The natural law is promulgated by the very fact that God instilled it into man's mind so as to be known by him naturally',[13] Locke did not believe it was in our minds at

---

[10] Richard Tuck, 'The "modern" theory of natural law', in *The Languages of Political Theory in Early Modern Europe*, ed. Anthony Pagden (Cambridge: Cambridge University Press, 1987), p. 112.

[11] Ibid., p. 113.

[12] In Locke's *Essay Concerning Human Understanding* we are told that the natural law is not composed of 'innate principles' written on the hearts of men. Rather, it is by reason operating upon empirically observed phenomena that men come to know the natural law. Locke is quite clear that we identify the content of the natural law through rational reflection upon ideas that we have acquired through experience. In the same way that, by experience, we acquire the idea of a triangle and subsequently extrapolate geometrical truths using our reason, we can similarly acquire a conception of man and, using reason, arrive at a knowledge of axiomatic truths regarding man and government. Furthermore, the natural law ceases to be an innate law, Locke telling us that 'There is a great deal of difference between an innate law, and a law of nature; between something imprinted on our minds in their very original, and something that we, being ignorant of, may attain to the knowledge of, by the use and due application of our natural faculties.' He believed that both those that 'either affirm an innate law, or deny that there is a law knowable by the light of nature, i.e. without the help of positive revelation' were mistaken and 'forsake the truth'.

[13] Thomas Aquinas, *Summa Theologica: Prima Secundae Partis*, trans. Fathers of the English Dominican Province in: *Christian Classics* (Notre Dame, 1981), Q. 90, A. 4. In the *Second Treatise* we shall see that Locke's understanding of the natural law is not straightforward. While Waldron has quickly pointed out that it is a theological account, he has perhaps passed over too quickly the fact that it is 'demonstrative in form, on issues such as property, punishment and politics.' Locke does indeed, at points, offer relatively orthodox descriptions of the natural law as a God-ordained standard of right and wrong in the *Second Treatise*. Yet, as we shall see, this is not Aquinas' natural law which, in its primary precepts, 'can nowise be blotted out from men's hearts.'

all.[14] Locke certainly did not believe it to be actively ordering all creation to its proper ends. Aquinas believed the natural law animated the whole of our human nature, when our nature was ordered as it was created to be ordered, namely in accordance with divine reason. In the *Summa* he writes, 'All the inclinations of any parts whatsoever of human nature, e.g. of the concupiscible and irascible parts, in so far as they are ruled by reason, belong to the natural law'.[15] By contrast, Locke presents the natural law as the capacity of reason to discover axiomatic ideas through the observation of nature. The implication of this shift for the modern world is significant insofar as Locke was intentionally minimising the necessity of substantial articles of religious faith to a stable and just society. The key to this was making man and man's reason the origin of justice and civil concord. No longer was the natural law something extraneous given to us, but rather it was an idea given to us by our own reason. The most important work in understanding the foundations of our modern liberal society is John Locke's *Second Treatise of Government*.

The Second Treatise of Government examined

Locke's overarching objective is summarised neatly in the preface of the *Second Treatise* as he states, 'The latter is an essay concerning the *true* original extent and end of civil government'.[16] With this objective in mind, Locke begins by telling us what he believes the right role of government consists in.

Locke takes the very essence of political power:

---

[14] Interestingly Locke's contemporaries weren't convinced that his account of the law of nature was orthodox. In 1690, Tyrell and 'some thinking men at Oxford', were to find Locke's account of the law of nature troubling. In 1692 Tyrell sent Locke a book he had authored on the natural law with an accompanying note expressing his hope that the work gave 'the world a better account of the Law of Nature, and its obligation than what hath been already performed' in order to refute the doctrines of Hobbes. As Laslett writes 'Tyrell was not satisfied with what had been said on natural law in that work [*Two Treatises of Government*] or in the *Essay on Human Understanding*, and felt that Hobbes had still to be confounded'.

[15] Thomas Aquinas, *Summa Theologica: Prima Secundae Partis*, trans. Fathers of the English Dominican Province in: *Christian Classics* (Notre Dame, 1981). Q. 94, A. 2.

[16] Ashcraft, *Locke's Two Treatises*, op. cit., p. 3.

to be a right of making laws, with penalties of death, and consequently all less penalties for the regulating and preserving of property, and of employing the force of the community in the execution of such laws, and in the defence of the commonwealth from foreign injury, and all this only for the public good.[17]

From the outset we can see the centrality of property to Locke's political thought. We shall see that the idea that man is endowed with an inalienable right to the property of his own person will be axiomatic to Locke's political project and to the liberal tradition which follows him. Continuing to explore the idea of political power, Locke tells us that 'To understand political power aright... we must consider what estate all men are naturally in'. This statement is significant insofar as Locke supposes that the nature of political power can be deduced from a precise definition of man in his natural state. Locke argues that in the state of nature humans are in 'a state of perfect freedom to order their actions, and dispose of their possessions and persons as they think fit, within the bounds of the law of Nature, without asking leave, or depending upon the will of any other man'.[18] This optimistic assessment of man will be deeply significant for the tradition.

In addition to his account of man's natural state, Locke identifies a law of nature which gives bounds to the liberty of the state of nature. This begs the crucial question as to what Locke means by the law of nature and what it consists in. The answer is soon provided. Locke writes: 'The *state of nature* has a law of nature to govern it, which obliges every one: and reason, which is that law, teaches all mankind, who will but consult it, that being all *equal and independent,* no one ought to harm another in his life, health, liberty, or possessions'. In this way Locke asserts a natural equality in the state of nature as well as a natural right to life, health, liberty and possessions. For Locke, this conception of man is 'evident' from reason. Such beliefs have become common in our modern world and few in the West question *why* we take these natural rights for granted. In Locke's day this was not the case. Locke needed to provide some evidence for these rights that all reasonable people could agree

---

[17] Ibid., p. 8.
[18] Locke, *Second Treatise* in Ashcraft, *Locke's Two Treatises*, op. cit., p. 8.

upon. Locke argues that the reason it is self-evident that no one ought to harm others in their life, health, liberty, or possessions is that all humans are 'the workmanship of one omnipotent and infinitely wise Maker; all the servants of one sovereign Master, sent into the world by His order and about His business; they are His property.'[19]

For Locke then, the law of nature is reason itself, and it allows us to identify certain fundamentally held rights which logically follow from the idea of man in the state of nature. Locke deduces from his conception of man that 'there cannot be supposed any such subordination among us that may authorise us to destroy one another'. The claims that Locke is making act as the basic axioms from which his political project proceeds.

Locke's ideas about the natural state of man are important, since it is this same idea of the autonomous individual endowed with rights that remains central to the liberal political project to this day. It is significant that the liberal tradition sees mankind, at its most basic, as rational and virtuous. By contrast, premodern natural law thinkers maintained the Christian doctrine of original sin. The liberal understanding of human nature clearly affects the way the tradition approaches politics to this day. As one author notes, because liberals believe that humans are basically good, our modern liberal society has encouraged 'an explosion of freedom'. Quite intentionally, liberals have 'jettisoned' 'the weight of tradition, the strictures of religion and the shackles of custom'.[20] We shall see where this optimism in man's nature led the liberal tradition in the eighteenth century.

In Chapter V of the *Second Treatise* Locke's conception of man takes a significant step forward. Locke argues that by 'natural reason' we can know that men 'have a right to preservation, and consequently to meat and drink, and such other things as nature affords for their subsistence'. He reinforces this conception of man by arguing that it is also supported by revelation. We have already seen that men have natural rights because they are God's property, but Locke goes further. In a significant move for the liberal tradition, the rights are asserted as subjectively held individual

---

[19] Ibid., p. 9.
[20] John Marsh, *The Liberal Delusion: The Roots of our Current Moral* Crisis (Bury St. Edmunds: Arena Books, 2012), p. 30.

rights: 'every man has a property in his own person. This nobody has any right to but himself.' In short, aside from any theological claims, man *qua* man is endowed with certain inalienable rights. As Thomas Jefferson would later put it 'We hold these Truths to be self-evident, that all Men are created equal, that they are endowed by their Creator with certain unalienable Rights'. If this is beginning to sound similar to the rhetoric of Western leaders today, that's because it is.

These anthropological claims are axiomatic as Locke attempts to discern 'the ends of government'. Locke questions, 'If man in the state of nature be so free, as has been said; if he be absolute lord of his own person and possessions, equal to the greatest, and subject to no body, why will he part with his freedom?'. His answer is that it is 'obvious' that although in the state of nature man is completely free, he is constantly at threat and therefore his property is in jeopardy. As a result, men join into society with other men 'for the mutual preservation of their lives, liberties and estates, which I call by the general name, property'. From this he draws the conclusion that 'The great and chief end, therefore, of men's uniting into commonwealths, and putting themselves under government, is the preservation of their property.'[21] Here we see that from a conception of man as a bearer of property (including his person) Locke arrives at a deductive and, what he hopes to be, a theologically uncontroversial account of the right ends of government. Significantly, it is heavily focused upon the individual. Government is a creation of the people, beholden to the people and therefore it is the people's prerogative to dissolve it.

Throughout the course of the *Second Treatise* Locke continues deductively from his idea of the man in the state of nature as well as using scriptural authority and some historical examples as rhetorical tools to support his conclusions when necessary. The central issue with this deductive method is that, in abstractly defining the rights of man in the state of nature, Locke blurs the distinction between an abstract normative discussion (i.e. how we *ought* to think of humans) and a descriptive account of real humans in real political societies. The concern is that if Locke's idealised account of man is being used as the basis around

---

[21] John Locke, *Second Treatise on Government* (1690), ed. C. B. Macpherson (Indianapolis, IN: Hackett, 1980), p. 66.

which we build our ideas of government, we will end up with forms of government that are not fit for *real* people.

For example, in chapter VIII Locke discusses 'the Beginning of Political Societies'. He writes 'Men being, as has been said, by nature, all free, equal, and independent, no one can be put out of this estate, and subjected to the political power of another without his own consent'.[22] As a descriptive statement of the real world, this seems wildly optimistic if not plainly false. As David Hume commented in regards to the contractarian arguments, 'would these reasoners look abroad into the world, they would meet with nothing that, in the least, corresponds to their ideas, or can warrant so refined and philosophical a system'.[23] Yet this idealised idea of man in the state of nature is not incidental, but central, to Locke's entire project in the *Second Treatise*. It is the vision around which he builds his account of government and society and it is the means by which he arrives at fairly radical conclusions, such as the prerogative of the people to dissolve the government.

This lack of distinction between the ideal and the real was to be a source of real concern for Locke's critics, because they believed that the manner in which legal rights and liberties came about in particular societies really did matter. In their view, the actual story of British law and liberty does not start with free and equal men in the state of nature, it starts with bloody disputes against obstinate rulers.

A Letter Concerning Toleration

Locke's *Letter Concerning Toleration* is a more polemical work than his *Second Treatise*, but nevertheless the conclusions of his *Second Treatise* clearly underpin the discussion. Taken alongside the *Second Treatise* it gives us a key insight into the presumptions of modern liberalism. Before Locke's arguments for toleration were penned, he had already established that the legitimate end of government is preserving life and property and defending the commonwealth. It is unsurprising then that in *A Letter Concerning Toleration* (1689) Locke states, 'the business of laws is not to provide for the truth of opinions, but for the safety and

---

[22] Ibid., p. 52.
[23] David Hume, 'Of the Original Contract' (1752) in David Hume, *Essays, Moral, Political and Literary* (Basil: J. J. Tourniesen, New Ed., 1793).

security of the commonwealth and of every particular man's goods and person'.[24] This is again a statement which puts Locke at odds with earlier Christian thinkers. It should also be noted that, whilst Locke is arguing for state toleration, he is also extending a wider argument for the rationality of toleration in society more broadly, or as he puts it, for 'the mutual toleration of Christians in their different professions'.[25] Whilst there are different ways of dissecting Locke's argument, there are, broadly speaking, three different phases. The first thrust of Locke's argument casts doubt upon the intentions of those who favour persecution and asserts that establishing the just bounds between religion and the state is critical. The second phase sets about the task of establishing these just bounds, delineating the state's jurisdiction and the Church's jurisdiction. The final and longest phase of the argument attempts to address the practical outworking of Locke's theory, particularly in regard to ecclesial concerns.

It is important to note the reasons that Locke offers for establishing the 'just bounds' between the Church and the state. The primary reason lies in the fraudulent utilisation of civic or religious loyalties for private ends. This pertains equally to those who would seek to persecute 'with the pretence of care of the public weal' and those who would seek 'impunity for libertinism and licentiousness' on religious grounds.[26] Locke is attempting to find a secure solution which will guard against such persecution on the basis of religious belief. As in the *Second Treatise*, his understanding of natural rights in the state of nature will prove axiomatic in this project.

Having established that the 'just bounds' need to be delineated, Locke embarks upon this task. In this second phase of the argument he defines the commonwealth as 'a society of men constituted only for the procuring, preserving, and advancing their own civil interests', defining civil interests as 'life, liberty, health, and indolency of body; and the

---

[24] John Locke, *A Letter Concerning Toleration* (Huddersfield: J. Brook, 1796), p. 48.
[25] Ibid., p. 5.
[26] In John Perry's book *The Pretenses of Loyalty*, he identifies this passage as one of central importance in understanding the difficulties with Locke's liberalism. I shall turn to Perry's analysis shortly. John Perry, *The Pretenses of Loyalty* (Oxford University Press, 2011).

possession of outward things'.[27] The magistrate's role is then to rule over the 'impartial execution of equal laws, to secure unto all the people in general and to every one of his subjects in particular the just possession of these things'.[28] We might note how Locke has subtly concluded the right function of the magistrates in a manner which makes his conclusions seem completely uncontroversial. Locke is careful to couch his language in reasonable terms. Furthermore, as Perry notes, 'he presents even his most contested theological claims as "common sense"[29] when in fact 'he was taking sides on disputed theological questions'.[30]

Locke proceeds in this second phase of argument, stating 'let us now consider what the Church is'. Locke's definition of the Church is 'a voluntary society of men, joining themselves together of their own accord in order to the public worshipping of God in such manner as they judge acceptable to Him'. The term 'voluntary' is important in this definition. Locke is clear that men must be able to follow their own convictions and it is therefore for individuals to best determine their own salvation and their own Church. He envisions that 'ecclesiastical liberty will be preserved on all sides, and no man will have a legislator imposed upon him but whom himself has chosen'.

Locke attacks the notion that a Church cannot be a true Church unless it is institutional, noting 'how great have always been the divisions amongst even those who lay so much stress upon the Divine institution', arguing that appealing to orthodoxy is absurd because 'every church is orthodox to itself'[31] and 'The decision of that question belongs only to the Supreme judge of all men.'[32] In emphasising this epistemological divide, Locke defers judgment to God. In doing so he establishes the just bounds between the Church and the state, since it is only civic crimes which are epistemologically discernible and so the Church has no role in punishment. As voluntary societies, churches are solely in charge of their own affairs, 'no church is bound, by the duty of toleration, to retain any such person in her bosom as, after admonition, continues obstinately

---

[27] Locke, *A Letter Concerning Toleration*, op. cit., p. 10.
[28] Ibid., p. 11.
[29] Perry, op. cit., p. 108.
[30] Ibid.
[31] Locke, *A Letter Concerning Toleration*, op. cit., p.21.
[32] Ibid., p. 22.

to offend against the laws of the society'. However, 'the execution thereof' must 'carry with it no rough usage of word or action whereby the ejected person may any wise be damnified in body or estate. For all force (as has often been said) belongs only to the magistrate'.[33] In this way Locke neatly divides society into two separate spheres, in the belief that should each 'contain itself within its own bounds — the one attending to the worldly welfare of the commonwealth, the other to the salvation of souls — it is impossible that any discord should ever have happened between them'.[34] In this statement it is not hard to discern the beginnings of the liberal secular state in which religion remains a matter of private belief. To be sure, Locke himself was not seeking a secular society, but it was an intellectual move which was advanced by subsequent generations of liberal thinkers.

Crucially, at this juncture we should note the importance of natural rights as the dividing line between the 'just bounds' of Church and state. Locke is clear that a sin is not the concern of the state if it is not in violation of an individual's rights. He tells us: 'Covetousness, uncharitableness, idleness, and many other things are sins by the consent of men, which yet no man ever said were to be punished by the magistrate. The reason is because they are not prejudicial to other men's rights, nor do they break the public peace of societies'.[35] Within the first few pages of his letter, Locke has seemingly achieved a golden formula for civil peace. The Church and the state are concerned with distinct jurisdictions and there is an ostensibly clear rule, rooted in natural rights, for differentiating between the jurisdictions. To give a modern example, in 2006, a British Airways employee, Nadia Eweida, was refused the right to wear a cross at work. The legal cases (finally ending at the European Court of Human Rights) were decided according to whether or not it constituted a violation of her human rights. In other words, the acceptability of the act was adjudicated upon, not according to cultural custom, but human rights.

[33] Ibid., p. 19.
[34] Ibid., p. 65.
[35] Ibid., p. 43.

Locke's jurisdictions jeopardised

Upon the basis of natural property rights and the equality of men, Locke defined the ends of government and insisted on the importance of civil toleration between religious groups. Yet, what Locke does not seem to take full account of is that, in the messy realm of human motivations, separating the business of Government from the business of religion amounts to an impossible task. John Perry's *The Pretenses of Loyalty* is concerned with precisely this issue in Locke's thought. Perry points out that Locke was attempting to address a central problem: that citizens 'usually take up their religion in gross, and assume to themselves the opinions of their party all at once in a bundle'.[36] Perry draws attention to the fact that 'Locke's intellectual quest was for a massive debundling'[37] in order to establish civic peace and toleration. As we have seen in his *Letter Concerning Toleration*, it was for this reason that Locke deemed it necessary to establish the correct divisions of the Church and the state. Yet Locke's optimism seems ill founded when one reflects upon the simple fact that religious viewpoints clearly do have political implications. Few instances in history have illustrated this point more clearly than the Wars of Religion which followed the Reformation. If one ceases to believe in the Doctrine of Papal Supremacy then this will have radical implications for the polity. As Perry points out, 'sometimes things *do* come in bundles'.[38]

Locke consistently attempts to avoid the conclusion that in disputed cases the state may need to take its own theological character seriously, as well as avoiding the conclusion that there may be an irresoluble tension between an individual's religious and civic loyalties. The state is not in fact a neutral arbitrator, but necessarily has its own ethical and indeed theological values so the citizen is at times confronted with a clash of civic and religious duties. To give a modern example of this, we can look at the banning of the burka in France in 2010. The burka was banned because of a set of moral beliefs which the state holds about the dignity of women. The state is not a neutral arbiter (as much as Locke hoped

---

[36] John Locke, *Political Essays*, ed. Mark Goldie (New York, NY: Cambridge University Press, 1997), p. 146.
[37] Perry, op. cit., p. 128.
[38] Ibid., p. 129.

it could be), but has its own distinctive set of values ultimately derived from metaphysical beliefs about the human person. By the same token, those Muslims who feel a strong religious imperative to wear the burka cannot simply separate their religious and civic values. And herein lies one of the fundamental problems faced by modern liberal democracies: they have forgotten that their own beliefs are theological in nature and not simply the product of reason. The idea of human beings as bearers of natural rights is not a theologically neutral position. The state makes judgements as to which expressions of religion are acceptable in the public sphere according to its own theological account of humans as rational, autonomous beings who are equal and bearers of natural rights. In issues in which the one jurisdiction encroaches upon the other, Locke's political jurisdictions break down and the possibility of conflict between state and citizens arises.

Locke's theological roots

Once he has established the existence of natural rights, Locke's framework is designed to seem coherent without Christian theological considerations.[39] Perhaps understandably, Locke's desire for toleration led him to avoid constructing his political framework upon a substantial theology, choosing instead a political framework centred upon natural rights. In doing so, Locke hoped to preserve a universal obligation for toleration and civic obedience, making them an obligation on the part of all people irrespective of personal theological convictions. Locke would not have foreseen or, in all probability, desired the appropriation of his philosophy without any reference whatsoever to the theological roots of his argument for equality and natural rights; nevertheless this is what we see in contemporary formulations of contractarian liberalism.

Jeremy Waldron and others have pointed out that the assertion of subjective rights is incoherent without the theological roots of those rights. This is entirely true, and we shall see how the modern liberal state has fallen into the false belief that it makes no theological claims and that natural rights are a product of reason alone. Waldron is also

---

[39] This is the central claim which Waldron would disagree with. See Jeremy Waldron, *God, Locke and Equality* (Cambridge: Cambridge University Press, 2002).

right to point out that when modern liberals assume their beliefs emerge from reason alone (as opposed to a distinct tradition), they would do well to remember that the belief in natural rights emerged from a Christian culture that professed the dignity of all humans. In other words, it was a distinct culture of theological belief that already existed which led Locke to posit the inherent worth of humans, not an *a priori* deduction. Yet what Waldron's argument does not emphasise strongly enough is that Locke's own theological commitments in the *Second Treatise* did not extend beyond grounding these subjective rights in a distinctively early modern form of the natural law.[40] In short, it is not enough simply to state that modern liberals have stripped Locke of his theology; we should also acknowledge that Locke denuded his own political thought of substantial theological commitments in order to make his claims more palatable to the factions of his day.

The impact of Locke's Second Treatise

What then was the actual impact of Locke's work upon British politics? The short answer is that Locke's liberalism had a limited impact upon British society and forms of government. Mark Goldie's six volume work *The Reception of Locke's Politics* provides an extensive insight into the impact of Locke's political thought in Britain, France and America in the eighteenth and nineteenth centuries. Goldie is clear that Locke's political thought was considered too radical by mainstream Whigs and, as a result, his writings were to have little serious impact upon British government following the 1689 settlement. As Goldie points out, by contrast to the flurry of tracts rebutting Hobbes' Leviathan, Locke's *Two Treatises* received relatively little attention until the second half of the eighteenth century.[41] Goldie writes that 'Even Whigs could find it disturbingly extreme.' He notes that 'The Convention which met early in 1689 – in all appearances an ordinary parliament – filled

---

[40] We can detect a nascent detachment of the Early Modern natural law from God when Grotius writes of the natural law, 'What we have been saying would have a degree of validity even if we should concede that which cannot be conceded without the utmost wickedness, that there is no God, or that the affairs of men are of no concern to him.' Hugo Grotius, *De jure belli ac pacis libri tres,* Prolegomena, II, trans. Francis W. Kelsey in J. B. Scott (ed.), *The Classics of International Law* (Oxford: Clarendon Press, 1925).

[41] Goldie, op. cit., p. xxii.

the 'vacancy' in the throne, leaving institutions of monarchy and the "ancient constitution" virtually untouched.'[42] This 'cautious' view of the revolution as a fundamentally conservative act was precisely the view that Burke held. Pamphlets of the time support the view that the revolution was primarily justified according to established laws and the ancient constitution as opposed to an abstract doctrine of right. William Atwood wrote that he was 'assured by Learned Men in the Law, whom I have consulted' that 'King *William* and Queen *Mary* are RIGHTFUL *King* and *Queen*, according to the ancient Constitution'.[43] Even Locke's close friend James Tyrrell was aware of the potentially revolutionary interpretation of Locke, and therefore 'aimed to make Locke safe' in his *Bibliotheca Politica.*[44]

Leading Locke scholars such as John Dunn and Francis Pocock agree with Goldie's assessment.[45] Richard Ashcraft tells us that 'the Whigs who came to power in the wake of the Glorious Revolution did *not* rush to embrace the ideas of Locke and Sidney, nor did they claim their writings as the canon of a "classical Whig" doctrine… most Whigs in the 1690s went to considerable lengths to disassociate themselves from the "dangerous" opinions contained in the *Two Treatises* and the *Discourses Concerning Government'*. [46]

Being highly familiar with British constitutional history, Burke would have been aware of such Whig reactions to Locke. Whilst the conclusions of Locke's *Treatises of Government* did not serve as a motor for revolution in Great Britain, the intellectual impact of his political thought was most significant in its effect upon the *philosophes* on the continent of Europe and the revolutionary liberals in the eighteenth century. In the initial years after the publication of the *Second Treatise*, both the Country Party and English republicans proved to be a more significant influence upon British society than the works of John Locke.

[42] Ibid., p. xxiii.

[43] William Atwood (1690) in Goldie, op. cit., p. 37.

[44] Goldie, op. cit., p. 64.

[45] John Dunn, 'The Politics of Locke in England and America', in John Dunn (ed.) *Political Obligation in its Historical Context* (Cambridge, 1980); J. G. A. Pocock, *The Machiavellian Moment: Florentine Political Thought and the Atlantic Republican Tradition* (Princeton, NJ: Princeton University Press, 1975).

[46] Richard Ashcraft, *Revolutionary Politics and Locke's Two Treatises of Government* (Princeton, NJ: Princeton University Press, 1986), p. 184.

What is certainly clear is that Locke has been subject to diverse usages. Perhaps his most significant legacy was to be a tradition of contractarian thought which took seriously a methodological approach to politics as illustrated in the *Second Treatise*. In the second half of the twentieth century Locke's ideas of natural rights, liberty and equality would see a remarkable resurgence in the West.

Chapter Three

Burke's critique of natural rights

In this Chapter we shall examine the objections of Edmund Burke to the approach to politics which Locke was advocating. Many of his arguments are still shared by contemporary conservatives in their objections to liberalism.

Burke articulated his arguments against contractarian thought over a century after the publication of Locke's *Second Treatise*. He did so in opposition to a prominent Lockean preacher who extolled the virtues of the French Revolution. As we have seen, the seventeenth century saw a wellspring of prominent thinkers arguing for the construction of a grand system of knowledge deduced rationally from first principles. Burke contended very simply that a society ought not to be reconstituted on the basis of ostensibly held natural rights. Burke believed that the strength of a robust political system, such as that possessed by the British, is that it is ancient, evolving and apposite to its own specific context. He argued that the liberal champions of reason often neglect the history and context of a nation that mould its political character, favouring instead an idealised vision of man and society. In his view, the idealistic attempt to reorder a society around the ideals of equality and natural rights may endanger the liberties and rights that people actually enjoy. To illustrate the point, one might reflect on the British military intervention in Libya in 2011. Critics would argue that in the desire to bring an abstract idea of a democratic society built around human rights to the people of Libya, the British government, by expediting the collapse of existing structures of government, ended up jeopardising the few rights that the people of Libya actually enjoyed.

Locke's *Second Treatise of Government* is the type of deductive project which Burke was targeting. Firstly, the work is unconcerned with the historical narrative which is particular to the English nation; there is no mention of the charter of liberties under Henry I, Magna Carta, Simon de Montfort's rebellion, the Petition of Right or the progressive assertion of common law over the absolute sovereignty of the monarch. Instead of England's rich and convoluted history, we are offered a founding myth, a social contract arising from a state of nature. Underlying Locke's thought is an epistemology which prioritises the light of empirical reason and rational systems as opposed to the accumulated wealth of tradition. The link between Locke's epistemology and Lockean politics was one of which Burke keenly was aware, not least because Locke's epistemology came under criticism from prominent figures who were well known to Burke.[1]

Hume too was an important critic of Locke and his work was known to Burke. Despite substantial differences in other respects, Hume's critique of Locke's social contract and natural rights discourse was very similar to Burke's. Both men possessed a formidable knowledge of British history, which influenced their opinions on abstract theories of government. As Ashcraft points out '[For Hume] Political theory is thus grounded wholly in experience, custom and prudential action, and not in universalist moral claims regarding right or laws of nature... In order to grasp the meaning of politics, what is needed is "not any abstract theory of right" but an appreciation of the habits, prejudices, and the peculiar circumstances of the people.'[2] Like Hume, Burke questioned 'What were the rights of man previous to his entering into a state of society? Whether they were paramount to, or inferior to social rights,

---

[1] Sean Patrick Donlan has written the most comprehensive account of the impact of the Scottish Enlightenment on Burke. See Sean Patrick Donlan, 'Law and Lawyers in Edmund Burke's Scottish Enlightenment', *Studies in Burke and His Time*, Vol. 20, No. 1, (2005), p. 38. The Third Earl of Shaftesbury, a student of Locke's, was a serious critic of Locke's thought, which he believed to be devoid of moral and aesthetic values. For Shaftesbury it was the moral conscience instilled by God, and not an idea of other humans as rights bearers, which formed the basis of moral agency. His work was most probably known to Burke, not least because of Shaftesbury's account of the sublime. Shaftesbury was to be an influence upon the leading lights of the Scottish Enlightenment such as Francis Hutcheson, whose account of the moral sense of individuals and repudiation of Locke's innate ideas was also known to Burke.
[2] Richard Ashcraft, *Locke's Two Treatises*, op. cit., pp. 271-272.

he neither knew nor cared.'[3]

For Burke, any society was inevitably a product of so many contingent circumstances that it made no sense to speak of ideal forms of government without any reference to culture, climate, customs, geography and the innumerable factors which constitute a nation's character. Burke was clear that different forms of government would be suited to different people. It was on precisely these grounds that Burke rejected the enlightenment notion of an abstractly conceived polity which could bring an unending peace to enlightened men. He wrote that no theory related to human actions could be rightly assessed 'in all the nakedness and solitude of metaphysical abstraction. Circumstances (which with some gentleman pass for nothing) give in reality to every political principle its discriminating effect. The circumstances are what render every civil and political scheme beneficial or noxious to mankind.'[289]

In the twentieth century, the communist movement illustrated this point well. Abstractly conceived, the idea of a socio-economic order in which the means of production are held in common ownership, sounds utopian. Yet, when practised in the real world, it became apparent that such abstract ideas paid insufficient attention to the realities of the human character and the concrete circumstances of a nation. From Mongolia and Cambodia, to Ethiopia, Romania and Russia, the optimistic anthropology and idealised polity of Communism was responsible for more deaths (100 million)[4] than any other ideology in history. Long before twentieth century critics such as Milton Friedman or John Maynard Keynes, Burke saw the danger in abstract ideologies.

As a Christian himself, Burke was no ethical relativist in political affairs and he had no problem in adjudicating between better and worse forms of government. As we examine Burke's thought, it becomes

[3] Burke, in *The Parliamentary Register*, [1792] Vol. 33, p. 28. It is also no coincidence that admirers of Burke, such as Thomas Reid, were to offer serious criticisms of John Locke's account of human psychology. Whilst Burke was not a systematic philosopher, and both the form in which he expresses his thought and the content of his language are more proximate to Cicero or the common lawyers than to the leading lights of the Scottish Enlightenment, Burke would have been aware of these contemporary critics of Locke's psychology and the social contract theories of the seventeenth century.
[4] Estimate by the historian Stéphane Courtois.

apparent that there is a crucial distinction between sound political principles which are applied in concrete circumstances and the practice of abstractly proposing what *all* systems of government *ought* to look like.[5] Instead of the abstract theorising of the revolutionaries, Burke favoured prudence in political questions, 'Political reason is a computing principle: adding, subtracting, multiplying, and dividing, morally and not metaphysically or mathematically, true moral denominations.'[6]

The methodology of reform: Burke's solution

In the latter half of the eighteenth century, shortly before the French Revolution, Britain too underwent a growing agitation for reform. The rapid economic growth and expansion of the population throughout the course of the century had effected a political reaction which was felt in all strata of society, but particularly the urban middle classes. In the great urban centres of Britain a variety of clubs, societies and publications emerged. With 12.5 million newsheets being produced per year in 1775 and an ever increasing number of periodicals and pamphlets, a new age of popular information and political consciousness had dawned.[7] Furthermore, the American colonists' victory at Saratoga in 1777 had dealt a devastating blow to the British and the subsequent formation of the United States had given flesh to the radical idea of a republic. By 1782 Britain was in serious debt, humiliated and at risk of invasion from France. Domestic tensions were rising, as was concern at the prospect of an Irish rebellion. Unsurprisingly, there was an increasing desire for political reform in Britain.

Relatively moderate groups such as Christopher Wyvill's Yorkshire Association petitioned for parliamentary and economic reform; in this desire they were supported by the Rockingham Whigs. More radical

[5] Burke makes this point clearly when he writes, 'without the guide and light of sound, well-understood principles, all reasonings in politics, as in everything else, would be only a confused jumble of particular facts and details, without the means of drawing out any sort of theoretical or practical conclusion'. See 'Speech on a Motion for Leave to Bring in a Bill to Repeal and Alter Certain Acts Respecting Religious Opinions' (1792) in *The Works*, op. cit., Vol. X, p. 41.

[6] Edmund Burke, *Reflections on the Revolution in France,* op. cit., p. 126.

[7] H. T. Dickinson, *British Radicalism & The French Revolution 1789-1815* (Oxford: Basil Blackwell, 1985), p. 2. [296] See Anthony Page, *John Jebb and the Enlightenment Origins of British Radicalism* (London: Praeger, 2003), pp. 19-25.

societies such as the Wilkite *Society for the Supporters of the Bill of Rights*, led by John Horne Tooke, sought more extensive political change, as did radical figures such as John Jebb, an admirer of Wilkes who was greatly indebted to Locke in his political ideas, proposing radical republican ideas. James Burgh's *Political Disquisitions* is a good example of a radical work which explicitly articulates its debt to Locke.[8] It is no coincidence that figures such as Burgh met regularly with Price, Priestley, Franklin and other leading radicals in the 1760s. The theological beliefs of these radicals were an important influence upon their political views.[9] Many of the more radical and Lockean voices were Unitarians, Deists and other dissenters who associated reason with political reform and the toleration of religious dissent.[10]

Hampsher-Monk has pointed out the great influence which Locke exercised on Deism in the century that followed him, also making the case that Burke was well aware of Anglican arguments against the Deists, employing these arguments for his own purposes.[11] Similarly, Seamus Deane writes, 'the Dissenters developed their positions on these issues from a specifically English inheritance going back to Locke'. Deane rightly points out that, given that the French radicals were influenced by the same source, 'the coincidence between these two groups is not altogether surprising.'[12] Unsurprisingly, the British Jacobinism which would emerge in the 1790s would predominantly find support among such groups, with organisations such as *The Revolution Society* pressing for a repeal of the Test and Corporation Acts on Lockean grounds.[13]

We have seen that the common lawyers coupled the natural law with

---

[8] James Burgh, *Political Disquisitions* (London: E. and C. Dilly, 1775), p. vii.

[9] A good analysis of the importance of Dissenters to the American Revolutionary cause in Britain is provided in J. C. D. Clark, *The Language of Liberty* (Cambridge: Cambridge University Press, 1994).

[10] See Ibid., pp. 334-335.

[11] Hampsher-Monk also makes the point that Locke was well aware of the Anglican arguments against the Deists. See Iain Hampsher-Monk, 'Burke and the Religious Sources of Skeptical Conservatism', in Iain Hampsher-Monk (ed.), *Edmund Burke* (Farnham: Ashgate, 2009).

[12] Seamus Deane, *The French Revolution and Enlightenment in England* (London: Harvard University Press, 1988), p. 159.

[13] The Society of Constitutional Information was a close affiliate of the Revolution Society and was revived in 1790. In the same year one of its members, Henry Flood, introduced a motion for parliamentary reform.

the ancient constitution, the one informing the other. By contrast, the proponents of radical natural rights believed such rights had the authority to overturn ancient institutions. Natural rights were being elevated above historically grounded legal rights.[14] Seamus Deane writes, 'from the early 1760s the influence of Locke, or at least of natural-rights arguments building upon aspects of his thought, revived with a vengeance'.[15] Similarly, the historian H.T. Dickinson writes, 'The leading radical theorists however tended to abandon an appeal to history and stressed instead the natural and inalienable rights of all men. They... built upon the earlier rational theories of John Locke and Richard Price who had asserted the natural rights of all men.'[16] As Burke himself put it, they argued on the 'claim of right, on the supposed rights of man as man', proceeding to complain that 'Nine tenths of the Reformers argue thus, that is on the natural right'.[17]

It should be remembered that between 1779 and 1780 Burke himself had been campaigning tirelessly for economic reform and had directly opposed his patron Rockingham, an owner of Irish land, in supporting the rights of Catholic Irishmen against the oppression of the Protestant (and Whiggish) Irish Volunteers, even putting his own career at risk by supporting the Irish Trade Bills.[18] Furthermore, Burke and the Rockingham Whigs were themselves in favour of reform, arguing that the problem lay in the excessive influence of Crown patronage, Burke having laid out his plans for economic reform in 1780. This shows that Burke cannot easily be characterised as a reactionary opposing any type of reform. Burke was deeply critical of claims to an inherent natural right because they abrogated the particular rights bequeathed by British tradition.

Following the fall of Lord North's government in 1782, William Pitt the Younger made a motion in the Commons for an inquiry into the geographical distribution of parliamentary seats. This occasion prompted

---

[14] Wilfred Prest, *Albion Ascendant: English History 1660-1815* (New York, NY: Oxford University Press, 1998), p. 280.

[15] Deane, op. cit., p. 159.

[16] Dickinson, op. cit., p. 14.

[17] Burke 'Speech on the Reform of the Representation in the House of Commons', *The Works*, op. cit., Vol. X, p. 95.

[18] See Burke's 'Speech on Economical Reform', *The Works,* op. cit., Vol. III.

Burke's undelivered 'Speech on the Reform of the Representation of the Commons in Parliament' (1782) (the 'Speech'). Burke's sentiments in the Speech could hardly be summarised more concisely than by Benjamin Disraeli's quip: 'To the liberalism they profess, I prefer the liberties we enjoy; to the Rights of Man, the rights of Englishmen'. In the Speech Burke spoke with scorn of 'political architects' who tried to rewrite the 'Constitution of England, which for a series of ages had been the proud distinction of this Country'. Burke contended that 'neither *now,* nor at *any* time, is it prudent or safe to be meddling with the fundamental principles, and ancient tried usages of our Constitution'.[19] He wrote:

> A prescriptive Government, such as ours, never was the work of any Legislator, never was made upon any foregone theory. It seems to me a preposterous way of reasoning, and a perfect confusion of ideas, to take the theories, which learned and speculative men have made from that Government, and then supposing it made on those theories, which were made from it, to accuse the Government as not corresponding with them.[20]

As Roger Scruton puts it, 'in defending this old view, Burke demonstrated that it was a far more effective guarantee of the liberties of the individual than the new idea, which was founded in the promise of those very liberties, only abstractly, universally, and therefore unreally defined. Real freedom, concrete freedom, the freedom that can actually be defined, claimed, and granted, was not the opposite of obedience but its other side.'[21] Burke coupled this instinct to preserve all that was good with the insistence that those deficient parts of a society should be identified and improved. As a tireless campaigner for social reform himself, he claimed that the standard of a good statesmen is 'a disposition to preserve and an ability to improve'. He did not seek to improve society because of a belief in a general natural right, but because he considered the demands of divine justice and God's moral law to be paramount.

---

[19] Burke, 'On the Reform of Representation in the House of Commons', *The Works,* op. cit., Vol. X, p. 93.
[20] Ibid., p. 99.
[21] Roger Scruton, 'Why I Became a Conservative' in Mark Dooley (ed.), *The Roger Scruton Reader* (London: Continuum, 2009), p. 11.

Given the close association of Locke's name with a particular brand of contemporary radical thought, it is understandable that Burke hardly mentioned Locke. As Peter Stanlis rightly points out:

> Burke's opponents who attacked him from the assumption of revolutionary "natural rights" were generally well aware that they were in the political tradition of Locke. In 1793 the Constitutional Society of Sheffield printed an abstract of Locke's *Treatise on Civil Government*, the preface of which stated: "Edmund Burke, the Knight Errant of Feudality, declared in the House of Commons, that 'Locke's Treatise on Civil Government, was the worst book ever written.' We are certain it needs no further recommendation."[22]

Whilst there is no direct record of Burke making this statement, it is significant that contemporary Lockeans clearly saw Burke as an opponent of Locke.

Burke's Speech shows that he was already formulating the sort of arguments which would later be deployed in the *Reflections*. In the *Reflections* he would lament, 'Is every landmark of the country to be done away, in favour of a geometrical and arithmetical constitution?'.[23] He writes that natural rights theorists 'wrought under-ground a mine that will blow up at one grand explosion all examples of antiquity, all precedents, charters, and acts of parliament'. He recognised that 'They have "the rights of men". Against these there can be no prescription; against these no argument is binding.' He saw that there could be 'no compromise' with such theorists, as if a government's 'forms do not quadrate with their theories' then they would turn against 'such an old and beneficent government as against the most violent tyranny'.

As in the modern world, the idea of natural rights was capable of being used as a sort of trump card to defeat any other argument from custom or common sense. As Burke observed, opponents of supposed natural rights were vilified as opponents of humanity itself. The issue was therefore as much about the *methodology* of reform as it was about the axioms according to which reform was to be wrought.

---

[22] Peter J. Stanlis, *Edmund Burke and the Natural Law*, (Transaction Publishers, 2015), p. 140.
[23] Burke, *Reflections on the Revolution in France*, op. cit., p. 113.

British rights and British liberties

In 1757, while still a young man in London, Burke endeavoured to write a history of England from Caesar to Queen Anne. Despite terminating the project at the year 1216, he boasted an impressive knowledge of British history. In the *Reflections* he traces the lineage of British liberty from the 'Magna Charta of King John' to 'another positive charter from Henry I', both of which were an reaffirmation of 'more ancient standing law of the kingdom'. He proceeds to offer an account of the Petition of Right under Charles I, carefully noting that 'the parliament says to the king, "Your subjects have inherited this freedom", claiming their franchises not on abstract principles "as the rights of men", but as the rights of Englishmen, and as a patrimony derived from their forefathers'. He then traces this lineage of liberties to the Declaration of Right under William and Mary, of whom he writes 'the two Houses utter not a syllable of "a right to frame a government for themselves". You will see that their whole care was to secure the religion, laws, and liberties that had been long possessed, and had been lately endangered'.[24]

Burke's conclusion is an explicit affirmation of the concrete historical tradition which had given rise to British liberties, and a rejection of general notions of right outside of any tradition. He tells us that from Magna Carta to the Declaration of Right, the British constitution has claimed the liberties of its citizens 'as an entailed inheritance derived to us from our forefathers, and to be transmitted to our posterity — as an estate specially belonging to the people of this kingdom, without any reference whatever to any other more general or prior right'.[25] In contrast to the 'sophisters', he claims that the British have 'chosen our nature rather than our speculations, our breasts rather than our inventions, for the great conservatories and magazines of our rights and privileges'.[26]

For Burke, history is not simply a forgotten past but it is an active inheritance. The cultural genome of a people forged in response to the exigencies of the past remains intimately present in the DNA of a society. The revolutionaries' abstractions were by contrast untested by the vicissitudes of time and turbulent circumstance.

It is, in part, this belief which grounds Burke's instinct to preserve.

[24] Ibid., p. 77.
[25] Ibid., pp. 77-78.
[26] Ibid., p. 80.

He tells us that 'it is with infinite caution that any man ought to venture upon pulling down an edifice which has answered in any tolerable degree for ages the common purposes of society, or on building it up again without having models and patterns of approved utility before his eyes'.[27] For Burke, the 'simple governments' created from abstract theory, are 'fundamentally defective to say no worse of them' and unable to answer the 'complex purposes' of actual societies.[28]

Burke's Social Contract

In 1789, Thomas Jefferson wrote to James Madison, 'I set out on this ground what I suppose to be self evident, "*that the earth belongs in usufruct to the living*": that the dead have neither powers nor rights over it'.[29] Burke challenged this early modern notion of the social contract by engaging with it on its own terms. He was arguing against the relatively new contractarian doctrines of the early moderns with the conception of the constitution articulated from the time of John Fortescue (who wrote his *De Laudibus Legum Angliae* (*Commendation of the Laws of England*) in the fifteenth century) onwards.

Burke tells us that 'Society is indeed a contract... but the state ought not to be considered as nothing better than a partnership agreement in a trade of pepper and coffee, callico or tobacco, or some other such low concern... to be dissolved by the fancy of the parties. It is to be looked on with other reverence'. It was to be revered 'because it is not a partnership in things subservient only to the gross animal existence of a temporary and perishable nature. It is a partnership in all science; a partnership in all art; a partnership in every virtue, and in all perfection. As the ends of such a partnership cannot be obtained in many generations, it becomes a partnership not only between those who are living, but between those who are living, those who are dead, and those who are to be born.' More than this, 'Each contract of each particular state is but a clause in the great primaeval contract of eternal society, linking the lower with the higher natures, connecting the visible and invisible world, according to a

---

[27] Ibid., p. 125.
[28] Ibid., pp. 125-126.
[29] Thomas Jefferson, 'Letter to James Madison, Sep. 6, 1789' in Julian P. Boyd (ed.), *The Papers of Thomas Jefferson* (Princeton, NJ: Princeton University Press, 1950), Vol. 15, p. 392.

fixed compact sanctioned by the inviolable oath which holds all physical and all moral natures, each in their appointed place.'[30]

In this definition of society Burke questions the legitimacy of any social contract which seeks to sever the legacy of those who came before us. Yet even more notably, he writes that society connects the visible and invisible world. It is precisely because society is greater than any one man or generation, indeed because it is accountable to Heaven itself, that we should not try and remake it in our own image. In this way Burke grounds the narrative of British history within a broader theological narrative. To use Burke's language, Britain's history is 'a clause in the great primeaval contract of eternal society'. From this conviction comes the belief that those who are alive should not break faith with those who have died. For Burke, if this contract to which the dead and living are party is to be taken seriously, then the nation's self-understanding and aims will inevitably draw deeply upon the nation's historical identity; and crucially, that historical identity is intimately related to the contract of eternal society, that is, to God's moral law.

Summary

In this chapter we have seen that Burke encountered the same deductive thought espoused by Locke in the radical reformers of his own day. While the mainstream tradition of Whigs had largely dismissed Locke's radical political conclusions or, like Burke, were overt opponents of Lockean thought, there was a tradition of natural rights radicalism which explicitly identified itself with Locke. Burke did not accept the axioms on which the Lockean radicals of his own day were seeking to found a society but, just as importantly, he did not accept the deductive methodology of the radicals. We have seen that Burke and others believed such a methodology would overturn the stable institutions and civil liberties which had been hard won by centuries of gradual change, much of which was inspired by Christian theological beliefs. In the next chapter we shall see that France had its own tradition of liberal contractarian thought which also found its roots in Locke's *Second Treatise*.

---

[30] Burke, *Reflections on the Revolution in France*, op. cit., pp. 183-185.

Chapter Four

The Revolutionaries and the *Declaration of the Rights of Man*

The French Revolution

In 1789 France was in the throes of financial crisis, primarily because of the ruinous Seven Years

War with Britain and its involvement in the American Revolutionary War. Louis XVI and the Bourbon Monarchy were unpopular and, by the spring of 1789, the rumblings of public discontent were becoming steadily louder. A series of peasant rebellions in the countryside, fuelled by a grain shortage in the spring of 1788, culminated in 'la grande peur' (the great fear), a general panic that took place between 17th July and 3rd August 1789. Yet these rebellions were largely ignored in Britain and it was not until July 1789 that Britain's gaze became firmly fixed on the events taking place in France. In May 1789 Louis XVI had tried to summon the first Estates General since 1614, but was fatally undermined when on the 10th of June the Third Estate broke away, declaring itself the National Assembly of the People and inviting the other two estates to join it. July 1789 was a turning point that saw an intensification of violence in Paris, which culminated in the storming of the Bastille on 14th July. Throughout the rest of the month the fever of rebellion spread throughout the country, the cry of popular sovereignty uniting peasants into militias. On 26th August the newly formed National Constituent Assembly published their 'Declaration of the Rights of Man and of the Citizen'. A series of radical social reforms soon followed. On 2nd November it was declared that the Church's property was at the disposal of the nation and non-compliant clergy were either exiled or executed.

In the midst of this social fomentation the French *philosophes* provided an intellectual discourse which served as a motor of revolution. Eric Hobsbawn writes, 'a striking consensus of general ideas among a fairly coherent social group gave the revolutionary movement effective unity';[1] 'its ideas were those of classical liberalism... To this extent "the philosophers" can be justly made responsible for the Revolution'.[2] Another commentator writes, 'That the French Revolution was caused by "philosophy" was affirmed by Lichtenberg and by many other German, Italian, Dutch and French commentators in 1789 and during the 1790s. The new revolutionary consciousness generated a powerful revulsion against "aristocracy", traditional ideas, and ecclesiastical authority'.[3] Burke himself was clear on the matter; to understand the revolution it was necessary to understand the ideological commitments of the *philosophes*. Writing of his *Reflections* in 1790 Burke stated, 'I thought that the scheme of their building would be better comprehended in the design of their architects than in the execution of the masons.'[4] As Stanlis puts it, 'All of Burke's opponents 'accepted Locke's optimistic state of nature, his common-sense simplicity, his theory of a revocable contract, of the sovereignty of will over reason and his mechanistic psychology of human nature... Locke was the chief source for the 'natural rights' theories of Burke's pamphleteer opponents.'[5]

Burke was deeply critical of the *philosophes*, in particular Voltaire, Helvetius and Rousseau. Above all, he criticised the elements of their thought which they had inherited from Locke, namely the social contract, the rights of man and the relegation of articles of faith to the interior of the soul.[6] Voltaire was a self-confessed apostle of Lockean political thought and Baconian empiricism. Rousseau's philosophy was distinctive in its Romanticism, but he was also deeply influenced by English contractarian thought and, in particular, Locke's understanding of the

---

[1] Eric Hobsbawn, *The Age of Revolution: 1789-1848* (London: Abacus, 1962) p. 79.
[2] Ibid.
[3] Jonathan I. Israel, *Radical Enlightenment* (Oxford University Press, 2002), p. 938.
[4] Burke, 'Letter to a Member of the National Assembly', *The Works,* op. cit., Vol. VI, p. 4.
[5] Peter J. Stanlis, *Edmund Burke and the Natural Law* (Transaction Publishers, 2015), p. 137.
[6] See Burke, 'Letter to a Member of the National Assembly', *The Works,* op. cit., Vol. VI.

social contract. Rousseau's influence upon Robespierre in particular was to prove profoundly important as the revolution progressed. The Lockean rights discourse (employed particularly by Thomas Jefferson, who was no admirer of Burke,[7] and Benjamin Franklin) was to have a strong influence on the Marquis de Lafayette, who had himself fought in the American Revolutionary war. Lafayette helped to write the *Declaration of the Rights of Man and of the Citizen*, with the assistance of Thomas Jefferson. After the storming of the Bastille, Lafayette was appointed commander-in-chief of the National Guard. The projects which occupied the leading *philosophes* in the decades preceding the French revolution had a profound effect upon its course.

Bearing in mind the Enlightenment project, initiated by Descartes and pursued by Locke, to create a comprehensive system of knowledge in which ideal forms of government could be known as precisely as geometrical figures, it is worth drawing attention to the *Encyclopédie, ou dictionnaire raisonné des sciences, des arts et des métiers*. Edited by Diderot, among the chief contributors were Rousseau, Montesquieu, Baron d'Holbach and Voltaire. The work can be seen as the consummation of the Cartesian project to unify all knowledge into a grand system of thought that is rooted in simple principles. In the preliminary discourse, d'Alembert tells us, 'As an *Encyclopedia,* it is to set forth as well as possible the order and connection of the parts of human knowledge', proceeding to note the difficulty of the task upon which the authors of the Encyclopedie were resolved: 'if it is often difficult to reduce each particular science or art to a small number of rules or general notions, it is no less difficult to encompass the infinitely varied branches of human knowledge in a truly unified system'.[8] Following his seventeenth century predecessors, d'Alembert is quite explicit in reducing the natural law to an anthropological axiom from which all other laws derive. For D'Holbach, the natural law consists in the right of men to preserve

---

[7] In a letter of 1791 Jefferson wrote, 'The Revolution of France does not astonish me so much as the revolution of Mr. Burke. I wish I could believe the latter proceeded from as pure motives as the former ... How mortifying that this evidence of the rottenness of his mind must oblige us now to ascribe to wicked motives those actions of his life which wore the mark of virtue and patriotism.' Thomas Jefferson, 'Letter to Benjamin Vaughan, May 11th, 1791', *The Papers of Thomas Jefferson*, Vol. 20, p. 391.

[8] Jean Le Rond D'Alembert, *Preliminary Discourse*, Vol. I, trans. Richard N. Schwab and Walter E. Rex, (Indianapolis, Bobbs-Merrill, 1963), p. 5.

themselves from death in a state of nature. Accordingly, men learn all other vices and virtues through social experience alone; neither revelation nor an active natural moral law are present.[9]

Similarly D'Holbach's *Système Social, Politique Naturelle* and *Morale Universelle* (all published in the 1770s) are a telling insight into the belief of the *philosophes* in the omnipotency of reason. In the preface to *Moralle Universelle*, D'Holbach tells us that 'Morality is a science whose principles are capable of a demonstration as clear and rigorous as those of calculus and geometry.' Again, we hear the early modern refrain, 'morality is founded on man's nature and his real interests, whatever his opinions or his prejudices'.[10] From this premise, D'Holbach proceeds to articulate a vision of society as dispensable and founded on the rights of the individual.[11]

From the 1760s onwards the *philosophes* were clear that they hoped to reform France in accordance with principles of liberty, equality and, above all, the 'rights of man'. Yet disputes between them were frequent and there was serious disagreement as to what form of government followed from the 'rights of man'.[12] Voltaire, for example, sought extensive reform of the state as opposed to the complete subversion of institutions espoused by Rousseau. Thomas Paine, on the other hand, sought a radical refashioning of the existing social order. In this sense, the French revolution was of a fundamentally different character to the American Revolution which was, in its origin, more concerned with rejecting tyrannical impositions upon the civil liberties of free born British citizens than in inventing new forms of government.

This was well illustrated in a dialogue between the French statesman Turgot and Dr Richard Price, a Welsh non-conformist minister who had written a popular pamphlet supporting the American Revolution. Turgot wrote to Price criticising the Americans for retaining an essentially British form of government. In a response, John Adams (later a US

[9] Ibid., p. 12.
[10] Baron D'Holbach, *Elements de la Morale Universelle, ou Catechism Universelle*, trans. Mitch Abador, found at:
https://www.marxists.org/reference/archive/holbach/1765/catechism.htm
(accessed, February 12th, 2014)
[11] Ibid.
[12] On this point, see John Lough, *The Philosophes and Post-Revolutionary France* (Oxford: Clarendon Press, 1982), Ch. 1.

President) defended the American retention of English customs, laws and, above all, an English form of government, precisely because it worked and was not in need of alteration.[13] Adams opposed Turgot's abstract talk of gathering all authority to the nation, writing that 'A simple and perfect democracy never yet existed among men'.[14]

While the *philosophes* advocated reconstituting the state in accordance with the principles of reason, this did not necessarily entail revolution. At least during the early stage of the revolution moderate revolutionaries such as Lafayette believed themselves to be reforming the state in accordance with principles of liberty and not completely subverting it. Yet the reformation was to be carried out in accordance with a vision of the state deduced *a Priori* from the *nouveau philosophie*. As Jonathan Israel puts it, 'France's existing culture of law and legal thinking had no input whatever. It is quite wrong to suggest that there was any trace of legal discourse or experience in the debates which were exclusively *philosophique* in character and in the decisive closing stages led by Mirabeau and Sieyès.'[15]

The desire to create a society founded upon reason and the Rights of Men made the revolutionaries familiar with the idea that reason was undermining the old dogmas of a Christian society. Rousseau's *Social Contract* is quite clear on this point. He tells us that, 'Jesus came to establish on earth a spiritual kingdom, which, separating the religious from the political system, destroyed the unity of the state, and caused the intestine divisions which have never ceased to agitate Christian nations.'[16] He proceeds to argue that Christianity and republicanism are mutually exclusive terms and that Christians 'are made to be slaves'.[17] For Rousseau, true religion is 'without temples, without altars, without

---

[13] See John Adams letters 'In Defence of the US Constitution' for his criticisms of the vagueness of the plans of reformers such as Turgot. See John Adams, *A defence of the United States of America, against the attacks of m. Turgot in his letter to Dr. Price, dated the twenty-second day of March, 1778*, Vol. I, (London: J. Stockdale, 1794).

[14] Ibid., p. 7.

[15] Jonathan I. Israel, *Radical Enlightenment: Philosophy and the Making of Modernity 1650-1750* (Oxford: Oxford University Press, 2001), p. 905.

[16] Jean-Jacques Rousseau, *The Social Contract* (1762), ed. Tom Griffith (London: Wordsworth Ed., 1998), p. 131.

[17] Ibid., p. 136.

rites, [and is] limited to the purely internal worship of the supreme God'.[18] As Israel puts it: 'Instead of drawing on Christianity, [Rousseau] thinks 'la volonté generale est le droit naturel' [the general will is the natural law], and that from society's 'volonté generale' all ideas of justice and morality derive.'[19]

In the light of such writings, it is easier to understand why Burke felt he needed to offer such an outspoken defence of Christendom. The link between the natural rights proponents and atheism was clear in his mind. He believed that the *philosophes* clearly desired the 'utter abolition, under any of its forms, of the Christian Religion'. He was infuriated that people could not perceive that 'the philosophical fanaticks' desired the downfall of the Christian religion, in the belief 'that they are able to supply the place of any good which may be in [religion], by a project of their own – namely, by a sort of education they have imagined, founded in a knowledge of the physical wants of men; progressively carried to an enlightened self-interest'.[20] Burke's fear that the enthronement of reason would in time produce an uncompromising attitude towards the imposition of faith into any matters of public policy proved to be well founded.[21]

The French revolutionaries and the Declaration of the Rights of Men

On 26th August 1789 at Versailles the deputies presented the *Declaration of the Rights of Men and of Citizens,* a document which served as the preamble to the constitution of 1791 and which stated the universal rights of men and the political implications of these rights. However, the French Revolution was a multi-faceted and complex event. Amongst the 'revolutionaries' there were a variety of factions with differing aims, ranging from reform to complete revolution. The National Party, of which Lafayette and Mirabeau were members, was on the more radical end of the reforming spectrum, although they were exceeded in their radicalism by some of the more extreme Jacobins such as Robespierre and the Abbé Sieyès. What is important is that the chief revolutionary figures who composed the *Declaration* believed themselves to be

[18] Ibid., p. 133.
[19] Israel, op. cit., p. 76.
[20] Burke, *Reflections on the Revolution in France*, op. cit., p. 270.
[21] Jonathan I. Israel, *Radical Enlightenment*, op. cit., p. 918.

overturning an old an unjust order and replacing it with a society founded on reason. They believed this reason to be grounded in the empirically established first principles of equality and natural rights. Jonathan Israel writes:

> By 1788 emerging Third Estate leaders already proclaimed equality the overriding moral and legal principle in legitimately determining relations among men. To them, the crown was irrelevant, the clergy's authority usurped, and nobility illicit. Their plans were moulded not by social class or experience, nor profession or economic interest, but a comprehensive, interlocking system of principles rooted in la philosophie, which, according to Mirabeau, Sieyès, Volney, Condorcet, and Brissot, was solidly anchored in empiricism and science.[22]

The revolutionaries believed their project to be something far more significant than just the reformation of France. As with modern liberalism, the project was essentially conceived as a transnational project. By 1791 the Girondist Jacques-Pierre Brissot had formulated a military plan to bring the enlightened liberties of the revolution to the rest of Europe. This ideal was a vision shared by British radicals across the channel. Richard Price and the Revolution Society, writing to the National Assembly in Paris, enjoined others to 'assert the *unalienable* rights of mankind, and thereby to introduce a general reformation in the governments of Europe' and 'make the world free and happy'.[23]

Repeatedly, we see the revolution conceived in transnational terms as a struggle for the liberty of mankind; Lafayette famously wrote, 'Humanity has won its battle, liberty now has a country'.[24] The liberal faith in the reason of mankind is well summarised in Jefferson's

---

[22] Jonathan I. Israel, *Revolutionary Ideas: An Intellectual History of the French Revolution from The Rights of Man to Robespierre* (Princeton, NJ: Princeton University Press, 2014), p. 26.

[23] Proceedings of the Revolution Society, *The New Annual Register, Or General Repository of History, Politics, And Literature for the Year 1789* (London: J. Robinson, 1790).

[24] See Janet Polasky, *Revolutions Without Borders: The Call to Liberty in the Atlantic World* (New Haven, CT: Yale University Press, 2015); Samuel Bernstein, *French Political and Intellectual History*, (New Brunswick, NJ: Transaction Publishers, 1984).

optimistic statement, 'I have so much confidence on the good sense of man, and his qualifications for self-government, that I am never afraid of the issue where reason is left free to exert her force; and I will agree to be stoned as a false prophet if all does not end well in this country. Nor will it end with this country. Hers is but the first chapter of the history of European liberty.'[25]

The *Declaration* itself was penned initially by Lafayette with influence from Mirabeau and Jefferson. Lafayette himself clearly conceived of the Enlightenment as instating a new order based on reason; 'The era of the American Revolution, which may be regarded as the beginning of a new social order for the whole world, is properly speaking the era of the declaration of rights.'[26] Similarly, in an early draft of the *Declaration*, Lafayette included 'The spread of Enlightenment' as a political aim. These human rights were clearly seen as objective in fact and universal in scope.

After several drafts, which were almost certainly revised by Jefferson, Lafayette completed the *Declaration* and read it as a 'profession of faith' to the National Assembly on 11th July 1789; the following day it was widely circulated around Paris. This draft was followed by proposals (with similar content) from a number of deputies including Sieyès, Target, Mounier, Rabaut, Mirabeau (and indeed the Sixth Bureau collectively) before the *Declaration of the Rights of Man* was passed by the National Constituent Assembly on 26th August after a week of discussion and voting.[27] The French Revolution is hard to comprehend without the admission that the key figures were seeking to replace the *ancien regime* with an enlightened constitution derived from the axiom that men are born free and equal. As Israel puts it, 'the Revolution's supporters conceived *la philosophie moderne* as the path to universal emancipation and happiness'.[28]

The *Declaration* contended that:

---

[25] Thomas Jefferson, 'Letter to Diodati', 3rd August 1789', *Papers*, XV, p. 326.
[26] Lafayette, "Sur la declaration des droits," Memoires, II, 303-4, in Margaret Madox and Louis Reichenthal Gottschalk, 'Lafayette in the French Revolution, through the October days' (Chicago, IL: University of Chicago Press, 1973), p. 85.
[27] William Doyle, *Oxford History of the French Revolution* (Oxford: Oxford University Press, 2nd Ed., 2002)
[28] See Jonathan I. Israel, *Revolutionary Ideas,* op. cit., p. 20.

> I. Men are born and always continue, free and equal in respect of their rights. Civil distinctions, therefore, can be founded only on public utility.
>
> II. The end of all political associations is the preservation of the natural and imprescriptible rights of man: and these rights are liberty, property, security and resistance of oppression.

It is striking that these first two articles could equally have been written by Locke. The structure of the project in which they were engaged seems to be nearly identical. Beginning with a normative assertion of the equality of men and the natural rights of men, they proceed deductively to the role of government. The first two articles of the *Declaration* alone show a remarkably strong conceptual similarity between the *Second Treatise* and the political project in which the intellectual vanguard of the French Revolution were self-consciously engaged.

In the last chapter we saw that Burke thought this species of deductive political science to be dangerous. Looking at the *Declaration*, it is not hard to identify the hallmarks of this same project. The preface to the *Declaration of the Rights of Man* is illuminating; the declaration aims to ensure:

> that the grievances of the citizens, based hereafter upon simple and incontestable principles, shall tend to the maintenance of the constitution and redound to the happiness of all. Therefore the National Assembly recognizes and proclaims, in the presence and under the auspices of the Supreme Being, the following rights of man and of the citizen.

The phrase 'based hereafter upon simple and incontestable principles' betrays the mode of deductive enquiry in which, like Locke, the French revolutionaries were engaged. The token nod to the 'auspices of the Supreme Being' both utilises Locke's language and draws upon a similar conception of the natural law to that employed by him. Notably, the *Declaration* avoids substantive theological commitments, simply invoking a divine authority which serves to ground the Rights of Man. The *Declaration* proceeds to present a political manifesto of seventeen articles which emerge from these first principles. It is striking that there is no reference to the *ancien regime*, to the existing government or to the culture and customs of France. It was because of this abstraction that Burke was led to admonish the revolutionaries, 'You had all these advantages in your ancient states, but you chose to act as if you had never been moulded into civil society and had everything to begin anew. You began ill, because you began by despising everything that belonged to you.'[29]

The lack of historical narrative or contextual considerations in the *Declaration* is well illustrated in its fourth article, concerning liberty:

> 4. Liberty consists in the freedom to do everything which injures no one else; hence the exercise of the natural rights of each man has no limits except those which assure to the other members of the society the enjoyment of the same rights. These limits can only be determined by law.

This definition of liberty, echoing both Hobbes and Locke, which proposes a 'freedom to do everything which injures no one else' is a good example of the abstract definition of liberty which troubled Burke and continues to trouble conservatives today. For Burke, such a definition of liberty could never hope to specify the myriad cultural customs, social relations and civic duties which constitute the complex texture of true human liberty: 'Abstract liberty, like other mere abstractions, is not to be found'.[30] He believed that the concrete liberty provided by a nation's longstanding laws would curtail the boundless freedom of the individual in one sense, yet it would ultimately provide a more substantial freedom.[31] As he put it, 'Liberty, too, must be limited in order to be possessed'.[32]

The fact that the revolutionaries spoke in terms of a universal liberty had a tangible effect on the way they viewed the traditions and history of a people. No longer were representatives the representatives of particular

---

[29] Burke, *Reflections on the Revolution in France*, op. cit., p. 82.
[30] Burke, 'Speech on Conciliation with America', *The Works*, op. cit., Vol. III, p. 49.
[31] This is a point Russell Kirk makes well. Russell Kirk, *Edmund Burke: A Genius Reconsidered* (New York, NY: Arlington House, 1967), p. 154.
[32] Burke, 'Letter to the Sheriffs of Bristol', *The Works*, op. cit., Vol. III, p. 185.

communities, but rather they were representatives of the general will.[33]

One might notice a paradoxical link between the radical assertions of individual liberty from the revolutionaries and the corporate tyranny of 'the general will'. Burke identified both excesses as different faces of the same coin. Both were permutations of unrestrained autonomy. The abstract elevation of reason, equality and the rights of the individual would, in Burke's eyes, inevitably result in corporate despotism. To offer a modern parallel, one might think today of the manner in which liberal culture is so focused upon the rights and equality of individuals, that points of view which seem to contravene them are sometimes denounced in what has been termed 'the tyranny of political correctness'. It was because of the connection between an excessive focus on the individual and the tyranny of the general will that Burke predicted 'some popular general, who understands the art of conciliating the soldiery, and who possesses the true spirit of command, shall draw the eyes of all men upon himself'.

In making this prescient prediction, Burke argued that when legitimate hierarchies of authority were displaced and excessive individualism elevated, the tyranny of rule by force would ensue: 'How came the Assembly by their present power over the army? ...They have destroyed the principle of obedience ...The soldier is told he is a citizen and has the rights of man and citizen. The right of a man, he is told, is to be his own governor and to be ruled only by those to whom he delegates that self-government.' This link between radical individualism and a strongly coercive corporate rule was certainly a link which Maximilien Robespierre perceived clearly; 'The general will rules in society as the private will governs each separate individual.'[34]

The Revolutionary conception of law articulated in the *Declaration* reflects this. Article VI begins with the blunt statement that, 'Law is the expression of the general will'. Rousseau can be credited with this phrase, and in such statements the revolutionaries went beyond Locke's liberalism. If this article seems to be an intentional affront to the belief that all authority emanates from God, we should not be surprised. Such a statement was intentionally aimed at repudiating notions of divine and

---

[33] Jonathan I. Israel, *Radical Enlightenment,* op. cit., p. 897.
[34] Maximilien Robespierre, *Lettres* à *ses Commettans*, Vol. 2, (January 5th, 1793).

monarchical sovereignty.[35]

The radical individualism of the revolutionaries is rooted in their conception of man as a solitary and rational creature. Their society was not modelled upon a vision of man as a socially integrated being, a dependent being, or a religious being. Burke's counter argument to this was that we should envisage human beings as we find them: in a society of established customs, particular manners, social bonds and religious feeling. He argued that many aspects of human existence which do not easily render themselves transparent to reason are a critical cohesive which bind together what he called 'the small platoons' of family and civil society.

The legacy of revolution

In April 1792 the French declared war on Austria, with Prussia joining soon after. As the French encroached upon Austrian territory in the Southern Netherlands, the British and the Dutch became increasingly concerned and joined the fight against the fledgling French Republic. On 17th January

1793 Louis XVI was condemned to death. Given what was to follow, there is a grim irony in the fact that the charge brought against him was that of conspiring against the public liberty. The shock waves following the King's execution reverberated around Europe. The financial state of France became increasingly untenable due to the war effort and there was a swell of popular discontent. Fearing a loss of control, the Jacobins seized power and formed the Committee of Public Safety in April 1793. The Jacobins began by arresting twenty-nine leading Girondins (more moderate revolutionaries), thus assuring their own political dominance. By the end of 1793 'the incorruptible' Robespierre had effectively become a dictator. The Committee of Public Safety had the Hebertist and Dantonist journalists who opposed them executed at the guillotine. On 21st October 1793 legislation was passed which ordered the execution of priests and any who harboured them on sight. On 24th October the Revolutionary Calendar was inaugurated in order to cleanse any remaining remnant of Christian tradition. These acts were accompanied

---

[35] Burke, *Reflections on the Revolution in France*, op. cit., p. 390.

by the sacking of churches and monuments, the prohibition of religious education and forced recantations of belief. In the place of traditional Christianity, Robespierre established the cult of the Supreme Being in a ceremony in Notre Dame Cathedral. In the first festival of the Supreme Being, Robespierre himself would descend from a man-made mountain in Paris, dressed all in white, as the chief prophet of the Supreme Being.

The 'Reign of Terror' between September 1793 and July 1794 is perhaps one of the most shocking features of the French Revolution. Sixteen and a half thousand people were sent to the guillotine with another 25,000 killed across France without any trial. A sizeable proportion of those who were killed were clergy and aristocrats, although the peasantry accounted for over seventy per cent of the deaths. In 1794 Robespierre purportedly made statements such as 'Terror is nothing else than justice, prompt, severe, inflexible', with the justification that 'it is supported by the most holy of all laws: the Salvation of the People'. France degenerated into a chaos which could only be quelled by further violence. Large scale revolts were mercilessly repressed, culminating in a massacre in the Vendée which claimed between 170,000 and 250,000 lives. The National Convention trampled on the liberties of its subjects using armed militias to extort grain from farmers and executing those who opposed the revolutionaries for 'crimes against liberty'. Ultimately Robespierre fell victim to his own violence and was himself executed without trial on 28th July 1794. A bankrupt and weary country would in time unite behind a strong dictator who could galvanise the nation, Napoleon Bonaparte. Yet this was not to be the end of the blood and violence in France since in the next century further turbulences, based upon revolutionary principles, destabilised the country.

It would be wrong to use the French Revolution as a simple vignette to illustrate that contractarian movements inevitably result in revolution and disaster. There are of course many contingent factors which shaped the course of the revolution: the grain shortages of the 1780s, the influence of *philosophes* such as Rousseau and Voltaire, the radicalism of leading figures such as Robespierre, and finally, a particularly obstinate and iniquitous ruling establishment. Nevertheless, the contractarian preference for natural rights and reason over ancient institutions was clearly an important element in providing the rationale for revolution. It is difficult to separate the revolutionaries' actions from the intellectual impetus offered by the *philosophes* and, according to leading historians such as Israel and Hobsbawm, we would be wrong to do so. Whether contractarian thought inevitably leads to violence or revolution is doubtful. That contractarianism intentionally provides a logic for the overthrow of established orthodoxies seems historically evident. At its best, it is a tradition that has boldly challenged grave injustices, yet at its worst it has brought a nation to its knees.

Lessons from the French Revolution
In this chapter we have looked at the contractarian thought of the revolutionaries. We have seen that Locke was the dominant influence upon the *Declaration,* and observed that the similarities with the *Second Treatise* are striking. In particular, we have seen that the axiomatic basis for the revolutionaries' political project, as well as the methodological assumption (that a perfect system of government can be rationally deduced), were both inherited from Locke. We have noted that the thought of Rousseau, Voltaire and other *philosophes* gave the *Declaration* a different character to the *Second Treatise.* While the same assumptions animated the core of the tradition, the atheism of the *philosophes* and, in particular, Rousseau's doctrine of the general will, gave the revolutionary movement a distinctly anti-clerical and corporatist tone.

In some respects there is a striking continuity between the liberalism of the revolutionary period and the liberal project today, to which we shall turn shortly. To give one example, the self-assured tone of liberals such as Jefferson is, in many ways, redolent of the tone of European technocrats today. The liberal belief that national boundaries, ancient institutions and cultural identities will inevitably be superseded by the inexorable march of reason seems so clear to European leaders such as Jean-Claude Juncker, who famously said of a national referendum on the EU constitution, 'If it's a Yes, we will say "on we go", and if it's a No we will say "we continue"'. EU leaders were astonished to find that the people of Britain had voted against the enlightened vision of the European Union. In the Brexit debate we can identify some parallels with the debate that took place in Britain two hundred years before.

Would the people of Britain favour a new integrated Europe founded on reason? Would Britain build a society around natural rights, freedom and equality, as laid down in a continental creed, or would it cling to the ancient institutions that had historically preserved its laws and liberties? In the eighteenth century it was the conservatives who won the debate. Chastised by liberals such as Thomas Paine, the British people favoured their existing laws and liberties over the rights of men and they favoured the Christian church over the church of reason. Ultimately, they would be proved right. The tyrannical rationalism of the liberal tradition would be its undoing. Those who disagreed with the reason of the liberals were no longer considered to be equals of the revolutionaries. As Napoleon's armies spread his 'enlightened' civil codes across Europe by the force of arms, it was Britain that would save the continent from his tyranny.

We can learn from French liberalism of this period that the revolutionaries' conviction that their form of government was derived from pure reason resulted in a remarkable intolerance, indeed a ferocious anger, towards religious groups. This was at a time in which explicit provisions were made for freedom of religion. As Burke pointed out, permitting a religion to exist only within the confines of what the liberal establishment deems reasonable can leave religious liberties in a very precarious position.

Chapter Five

John Rawls and Liberalism Today

Up to this point, we have looked at two different approaches to politics. First, we looked at Burke's approach, with its roots in the common law tradition, emphasising the operation of prudence, the circumstantial nature of government, and the importance of a Christian influence upon the culture of the nation. We have also looked at the liberal tradition originating in the seventeenth century, proposing subjectively held rights, a belief that the final authority is the general will of the people and the belief that the state ought to be the final arbiter over public affairs and society. But how does all of this relate to our world today? In this chapter we will look in the way in which contractarian ideas have come to dominate political theory and look at the most influential modern proponent of liberal thought.

The Liberal tradition in modern society

At the beginning of this book, I argued that there is an increasingly large divide between the assumptions of the liberal establishment and a variety of religious voices in society. We have seen how the liberal tradition emerged in the seventeenth century and developed in the eighteenth, yet we have also seen that its central ideas were perceived in Britain as dangerous and were largely rejected.

Over the last half century Britain has witnessed a decline in the Christian religion and a rise in the ideas of the liberal tradition. Most notably, we have seen a belief that citizens should be regarded as free and equal agents, guided by rational choice. Similarly, the state (and society more broadly) retain the vestiges of a Christian character, but few public decisions are made with any reference to the Christian faith. One of the predominant roles of the modern state is preserving the rights of citizens over and above the promotion of any particular conception of the good. This is in stark contrast to the Britain of the first half of the twentieth century, in which 'Christian values' were actively preserved by public institutions.[1] Conceptions of the good articulated by the state tend to be 'thin' values that all can seemingly agree on, such as tolerance, equality and a respect for human rights. These norms of the liberal tradition have become the accepted orthodoxy in our modern culture. But when and why did this change occur?

The sociological reasons for the transition to a more secularised and liberal public discourse are complex and disputed. Sociologists have variously cited the waves of mass immigration since the Second World War and the diversity of religions which this migration has brought with it,[2] the trauma of the war itself, the rise of technology and mass media, the differentiation of social institutions,[3] the egocentric consumerism of a capitalist nation,[4] or the conscious advancement of a secular liberal discourse by the liberal intelligentsia of the West.[5] The Universal Declaration of Human Rights, ratified in 1948 following the influence of liberals such as Franklin D. Roosevelt, can perhaps be pinpointed as a transitional moment in the refashioning of European laws and attitudes to the liberal discourse of human rights. Yet it is even more recently that the discourse of human rights and equality has come to affect the legal and political landscape of the United Kingdom. In 1998 the UK passed the Human Rights Act which incorporated the European Convention on Human Rights (1953) into British law. Since this time the Human Rights Act has given a code of rights to the citizens of the UK, helping

---

[1] Whether one looks at the numbers of church marriages, church attendance, religious literacy or references to religious faith in public life, all have declined rapidly since the 1950s.

[2] Steve Bruce, *Secularization: In Defence of an Unfashionable Theory* (Oxford University Press, 2013).

[3] P. L. Berger, B. Berger, and H. Kellner, *The Homeless Mind: Modernization and Consciousness* (Harmondsworth: Penguin, 1974).

[4] T. Luckmann, *The Invisible Religion: The Problem of Religion in Modern Society* (NY: Macmillan, 1967).

[5] Alasdair MacIntrye, *After Virtue: A Study in Moral Theory* (Notre Dame, IN: University of Notre Dame Press, 3rd Edition, 2007).

to reshape the legal landscape of the nation.

Whatever the causes, there has been, by broad consensus, a substantial shift away from a public Christian discourse in British society.[6] Alongside this, there has been an increase of a liberal discourse centred on equality and the rights of the individual. In the seventeenth and eighteenth centuries liberals hoped to create a society based on reason, centred upon the idea of humans as free, equal and bearers of natural rights. While liberals today are not literally tearing down infrastructure, as the French Revolutionaries did, they are reconstituting society by making equality, autonomy and natural rights the ultimate aspiration of our culture. To analyse precisely what the new liberal orthodoxy consists of, we need to examine the work of John Rawls.

John Rawls

John Rawls is undoubtedly one of the most influential thinkers of the twentieth century and his work on natural rights have been a major influence on ideas that are now common currency in the West. The Massachusetts Institute of Technology philosopher Joshua Cohen wrote 'His achievement in moral and political philosophy is certainly the largest achievement in the English-speaking world since John Stuart Mill's... his work has a place among the greatest tradition of moral and political philosophy and that would include Plato, Aristotle, Rousseau. I expect his work to continue to be studied for the indefinite future.'[7] The Harvard University President, Lawrence Summers wrote, 'Few if any modern philosophers have had as decisive an impact on how we think about justice.'[8] It is hard to assess Rawls' influence upon particular political parties or policies but, given the seminal influence of his thought upon a generation of thinkers, it is not hard to see how his work has percolated down to the level of policy. We may at least say that if the influence of rights and equality discourse is a barometer of influence then Rawls and similar thinkers of his generation have made a decisive impression upon political and popular culture. As Richard A. Epstein wrote 'Political

---

[6] It should be noted that there is significant dispute amongst sociologists as to whether the decline in public Christian discourse amounts to secularisation.

[7] Joshua Cohen, 'Rawls Remembered', in *The Philosophy Magazine*, Issue 22, 2003, p. 34.

[8] Lawrence H. Summers, in ibid.

philosophers, policymakers, and lawyers are all in the debt of [this] modest man'.[9] In short, Rawls' thought has underpinned much of the political discourse of liberal democracies in the early 21st Century.

Importantly, Rawls places himself in the stream of liberal thought which I have identified. He writes that he aspires 'to carry to a higher level of abstraction the familiar theory of the social contract as found, say, in Locke, Rousseau and Kant'.[10] In an accompanying footnote he tells us that 'I shall regard Locke's *Second Treatise of Government,* Rousseau's *The Social Contract*, and Kant's ethical works beginning with the *Foundations of the Metaphysics of Morals* as definitive of the contract tradition'.[11] Just as Locke's thought was conditioned by the work of Hobbes, Filmer and the current scientific ideas of his era, and the revolutionaries' thought was shaped by Rousseau and Voltaire, so Rawls has his own influences. The most important of these is Immanuel Kant.[12] If Rawls' work seems to make a conscious effort to avoid metaphysical claims, it is not a coincidence that his thought has been influenced by Kantian ethics which elevated reason above tradition and *mores*. Certain core features of Rawls' thought are remarkably similar to those found in earlier examples of contractarian thought and we see the capacity of the contractarian tradition to reinvent itself for a new generation.

Rawls's Liberalism – An Overview

In *Political Liberalism* [13] Rawls asks 'How is it possible that there may exist over time a stable and just society of free and equal citizens profoundly divided by reasonable religious, philosophical, and moral

[9] Richard A. Epstein, in Ibid.

[10] John Rawls, *A Theory of Justice* (Cambridge MA: Harvard University Press, Revised Ed., 1999), p. viii.

[11] Ibid., p. 10.

[12] Note that Rawls' interpretation of Kant is not undisputed. See Onora O'Neill, 'Constructivism in Rawls and Kant', in Samuel Richard Freeman (ed.) *The Cambridge Companion to Rawls*, (Cambridge: Cambridge University Press, 2003).

[13] See also John Rawls, *A Theory of Justice* (Cambridge MA: Harvard University Press, 1971); idem, *Justice as Fairness: A Restatement*, ed. Erin Kelly, (Cambridge, MA: Harvard University Press, 2001); idem 'The Idea of an Overlapping Consensus', *Philosophical Papers,* ed. J. Freeman, (Cambridge MA: Harvard University Press, 1999); idem, 'Kantian Constructivism in Moral Theory', *Journal of Philosophy*, 77 (1980), pp. 515–572.

doctrines?'.[14] This is a question which might sit happily in the preface to Locke's *Letter on Toleration*. The question provides the basis for a project of political construction which aspires to show 'that a certain arrangement of basic political and social institutions is more appropriate to realizing the values of liberty and equality when citizens are so conceived as free and equal persons'.[15] Like Locke, Rawls' starting point involves an abstract conception of man as free and equal; he tells us that '[political constructivism] uses a rather complex conception of person and society to give form and structure to its construction'.[16]

But we might note that, as in Locke's thinking, there is a distinctive, and self-conscious, absence of teleology in Rawls' account of the human person. Sandel notes this of Rawls' thought, and draws the link with the origins of contractarian thought, 'Only in a universe empty of *telos*, such as seventeenth-century science and philosophy affirmed, is it possible to conceive a subject apart from and prior to its purposes and ends.'[17] As with Locke, Rawls wants his political model to begin with a normative conception of free and equal humans who possess specifiable rights, since it is from these first principles that Rawls will construct his political framework. Yet, unlike Locke, Rawls does not offer a metaphysical vindication of this claim or reference a state of nature in which God created us.

In Locke's work we saw that one of the big challenges to which Locke was responding was how to arrive at an idea of justice without any reference to disputed religious positions. Rawls' work provides a novel solution to this problem. In order to establish 'reasonable principles of political justice'[18] Rawls employs an 'analytical device' which he terms 'the veil of ignorance'.[19] The veil of ignorance involves imagining an 'original position' in which society is recast and no individual has any way of knowing what circumstances they will occupy in the new

---

[14] John Rawls, *Political Liberalism* (1993), (Columbia Classics, 2005), p.4.

[15] Ibid., p. 5.

[16] Ibid., p. 93.

[17] Michael Sandel, *Liberalism and the Limits of Justice* (Cambridge: Cambridge University Press, 2nd Ed., 1998) p. 175.

[18] John Rawls, *Political Liberalism*, op. cit., p. 381.

[19] Ibid., p. 23.

society.[20] We can detect resonances of Locke's state of nature in this 'analytical device' yet, unlike Locke's state of nature, Rawls is not trying to vindicate a conception of man but is attempting to establish valid principles of political justice. Rawls believes that from this position we have 'all the relevant requirements of practical reason' in order to envisage a just society[21]. Rawls' substitution of the 'veil of ignorance' argument for Locke's state of nature seems a prudent move for the liberal tradition, since it not only dispels the problem of the historical validity of the state of nature, but also precludes any need for God in the argument.

Rawls calls his view 'justice as fairness'.[22] Rawls argues that using the original position we can identify two principles of justice that would regulate the institutions of a well-ordered society. In this way, a consensus can emerge in which society is 'a fair system of cooperation between free and equal citizens'.[23] The first principle of justice assures citizens of 'an equal claim to a fully adequate scheme of basic rights and liberties'.[24] He argues that all members of society should accept such a consensus as 'reasonable and rational' citizens. Rawls maintains that being 'reasonable persons', citizens should desire 'a system of fair cooperation' and that 'its fair terms be reasonable for all to accept is part of its idea of reciprocity'.[25] Being reasonable and rational similarly has implications for our comprehensive doctrines and the issue of tolerance. Rawls explains that 'the burdens of judgement – among reasonable persons – are the many hazards involved in the correct (and conscientious) exercise of our powers of reason and judgement'.[26] In other words, as reasonable individuals, an acceptance of our epistemic limitations and the contingencies of any moral decision should promote tolerance.

For the Burkean, this acknowledgement of limitations might be seen as a critical improvement from prior liberal thinkers. While Rawls retains a belief in abstraction and even makes statements which liken

[20] Ibid., pp. 23–27.
[21] Ibid., p. 90.
[22] Ibid., p. 11.
[23] Ibid., p. 22.
[24] Ibid., p. 5.
[25] Ibid., p. 50.
[26] 'Historical and social contingencies that are external to, and eventually undermine, their freedom and equality.' John Rawls, Ibid., p. 287.

his procedural constructivism to mathematics, taking stock of the burdens of human judgement in contingent circumstances *is* a part of the procedural application of Rawls' methodology. Despite the fact that Rawls aims to take Locke's abstractions to a higher level, he equally allows greater scope for accommodating those abstractions to particular circumstances. This development is broadly reflected in modern western liberal democracies, which have become less consciously fixated on the project of deducing a perfect political model, though no less concerned with creating a society according to a particular conception of the individual and no less convinced that the liberal democratic society centred on human rights is a universal archetype of what all societies *ought* to look like.

Rawls argues that the political conception of justice is perfectly compatible with different 'reasonable comprehensive doctrines' because there can exist an 'overlapping consensus' in a pluralistic society as 'the reasonable doctrines endorse the political conception, each from its own point of view'.[27] Whilst citizens are expected to support the principles of justice 'we do not assume they do so for all the same reasons, all the way down'.[28] This allows for citizens to have 'conflicting religious, philosophical, and moral views' and yet allows them to 'affirm the political conception from within different and opposing comprehensive doctrines'.[29] The significant caveat to this is that if an individual does not support the overlapping consensus, in other words, if an individual is seen to be unreasonable, they should be contained 'like war and disease – so that they do not overturn political justice'.[30]

In spite of such statements, Rawls argues that political liberalism is not itself a comprehensive doctrine, meaning it makes no metaphysical claims. Rawls argues that his conception of the person is a purely political conception. For Rawls, social unity is not based on any one comprehensive doctrine but rather on a 'consensus on the political conception'. Rawls hopes to appeal to a consensus among all citizens in the conviction that the right end of government ought not to involve any particular theological position. For this reason, Rawls is able to

[27] Ibid., p. 134.
[28] Rawls, *Justice as Fairness*, op. cit., p. 32.
[29] Ibid.
[30] Ibid., p. 64 (footnote 19).

argue that 'the political conception of justice is... a freestanding view'[31] which can be supported from within any comprehensive doctrine but is not itself indebted to any one comprehensive doctrine.

We can see beliefs and assumptions in these ideas that we find around us every day. Where once politicians and newspapers would make appeals on specifically Christian moral grounds, we now live in a world in which the vocabulary of public morality consists in a secular appeal to rights and justice that all can seemingly agree on. It is not hard to see how the logic of multiculturalism emerges from these ideas. It is also easy to see why such ideas run counter to the public privileging of any one religion, resulting in the interiorisation and relativisation of religious beliefs. For Christians, a key question is: if Christianity is only to have a public voice to the extent that it finds a common voice with Hinduism or Islam, then what remains distinctive about its message?

The Limits of Religion
We have previously noted that Locke responded to the issue of different religious claims by separating the claims of religious belief from the role of government. In this way, his political philosophy relied on the least controversial appeal to a creator of natural rights. The genius of Rawls' work is that he purports to find a novel solution to the initial liberal dilemma of facilitating peaceful coexistence whilst allowing freedom of religious belief. We have seen that Rawls has ostensibly constructed a political philosophy which has no need for an appeal to metaphysical rights. This neatly solves the issue of appealing to any one theological or moral position in order to affirm these rights. But what is the basis for what is considered reasonable?

Rawls' idea of overlapping consensus is employed not just to affirm constitutional essentials, but also as a way in which society can come to decisions concerning public affairs. Rawls proposes that political decisions should be made on the basis of reasons which are transparent to the common reason of other citizens and not on the basis of privately held beliefs to which other citizens would not consent. Rawls writes, 'To justify our political judgements to others is to convince them by public reason, that is, by ways of reasoning and inference appropriate

[31] Ibid., p. 12.

to fundamental political questions, and by appealing to beliefs, grounds, and political values it is reasonable for others also to acknowledge',[32] and he continues, stating that 'when the premises and conclusions are not acceptable on due reflection to all parties in disagreement, valid argument falls short of public justification.'[33]

Whilst Rawls' idea sounds like a reasonable compromise for opposing traditions, the central concern which has been raised by critics is that in reality Rawls' stream of liberalism is itself a comprehensive doctrine which takes precedence over any particular tradition, despite the fact that it works upon a purely political (and not a metaphysical) conception. Indeed, Rawls himself is quite candid about this. In a section of *Political Liberalism* entitled 'Permissible Conceptions of the Good and Political Virtues', Rawls frankly states:

> Justice as fairness is not procedurally neutral. Clearly its principles of justice are substantive and express far more than procedural values, and so do its political conceptions of society and person, which are represented in the original position.[34]

Therefore, insofar as the ideological tenets of liberalism act as the filter which arbitrates what other traditions are allowed to articulate, contractarianism does not just, as some have claimed, prioritise only a method of reaching decisions over a conception of the good, but does to some extent favour a particular account of the good. Rawls writes:

> Suppose that a particular religion, and the conception of the good belonging to it, can survive only if it controls the machinery of state and is able to practice effective intolerance. This religion will cease to exist in the well-ordered society of political liberalism.

Therefore, in keeping with what we have seen in earlier contractarian philosophies, the revealed truths of Christianity find their public limits within the contractarian account of man as a reasonable being who possesses natural rights.

[32] Ibid., p. 27.
[33] Ibid.
[34] Rawls, *Political Liberalism*, op. cit., p. 192.

Maureen Ramsay gives voice to the concern that Rawls' solution is not simply a fair means of arbitration between differing world views but the prioritisation of a more substantive liberal ideology. She is particularly concerned with the original position which provides the basis for public reason, writing that 'the original position is infected with the premises, concepts and values of liberalism'.[35] She proceeds to make a comment which could have been written by Burke: 'the asocial, atomistic, solitary, self-seeking free and equal person represented in the original position is so abstracted it is difficult to conceive of such a 'stripped down' individual being motivationally relevant to actual existing people'.

At first glance Rawls' theory may seem a striking innovation to the problem of engaging with ethical questions when people hold different religious and other views. Yet, there is an understandable anxiety that Rawls' liberalism only seems to offer a conditional promise of freedom to religious citizens, providing that in public they confine themselves to expressing and acting upon beliefs which accord with the premises of liberal contractarian thought.

Rawls remains within the tradition of contractarian liberalism which seeks to renovate the existing social order in accordance to a political model premised on an idea of the individual. He is a proponent of this position for similar reasons to Locke, namely due to the desire to maintain a peaceful order of justice between competing religious traditions. By contrast, rather than building a society around the idea of the individual endowed with rights, Burke argued that Britain already had a means by which matters of basic justice and constitutional essentials were established and it did not rest on what the *philosophes* believed to be reasonable.

Burke, Rawls and Justice

Burke's conception of justice is very different to that of Rawls. As we have seen, Burke presupposes a given order of justice which is immutably present throughout the universe and is impressed upon the minds of men. It is important to remind ourselves that Rawls does not preclude this possibility, yet neither does he endorse it; his project is purely political which, for Rawls, means not metaphysical. In Burke's

---

[35] Maureen Ramsay, *What's Wrong With Liberalism? A Radical Critique of Liberal Political Philosophy* (London: Leicester University Press, 1997), p. 114.

view justice is not, as Rawls would have it, a political notion of 'justice as fairness' settled by right reason without any reference to metaphysics or a particular religious tradition. Rather, Burke's account of justice is overtly metaphysical:

> There is one thing, and one thing only, which defies all mutation: that which existed before the world, and will survive the fabric of the world itself – I mean justice; that justice which, emanating from the Divinity, has a place in the breast of every one of us, given us for our guide with regard to ourselves and with regard to others, and which will stand, after this globe is burned to ashes, our advocate or our accuser, before the great Judge, when He comes to call upon us for the tenor of a well-spent life.[36]

As a part of God's eternal law, the role of justice in shaping the basic structure and constitutional essentials of a society is just as important for Burke as for Rawls. Yet Burke would have been disturbed by the idea that it is for us to conceive of the principles of justice and would have been even more troubled by the idea that this can be done through rational reflection alone without any reference to an authority beyond popular volition. Furthermore, we have also seen that Burke would be scandalised by the suggestion that creating the basic structure of society and a just constitution was our prerogative, instead believing that eternal laws of justice would shape society over generations through the operation of judicial prudence.

Popular Will and Political authority

A catalyst for Burke's *Reflections* was a sermon preached by Richard Price on 4th November 1789, entitled 'A Discourse on the Love of Our Country'.[37] In this sermon Price drew a comparison between what he perceived to be the principles of government which the British had voluntarily chosen in 1688 and the struggle in France to establish their

---

[36] Edmund Burke, 'Indictment of Warren Hastings' in Lewis Copeland, Lawrence W. Lamm and Stephen J. McKenna (eds.), *The World's Greatest Speeches* (USA: Dover, 4th Ed., 1999), p. 164.

[37] Price was a dissenting minister as well as a philosopher, a demographer and fellow of the Royal Society; he was also personally acquainted with Thomas Jefferson, John Adams and Benjamin Franklin, as well as Thomas Paine.

own political system.

Price troubled Burke because of his assertion that by virtue of our reason we are able to determine for ourselves the principles of right government and then simply install this system of government by an act of popular revolt. Price's argument implied that in the events of 1688 the British had forsaken the inherited constitutional principle of hereditary monarchy and substituted this kind of free choice.

Burke did not think that political arrangements should be the product of pure will; whether it was the will of the people or of the ruler, this was a doctrine which Burke rejected in the strongest terms.[38] Burke argued that there were fixed and inescapable moral duties which inhered within the constitution to which a nation was bound, and in his view the British people had not taken leave of these duties in the revolution of 1688. In his Speech on the Army Estimates, Burke tells us that 'the Prince of Orange... was called in by the flower of the English aristocracy to defend its ancient constitution and not to level all distinctions'.[39] He believed that the conduct of 'the whole English nation at that time' was completely different to that of the French. 'In truth, the circumstances of our Revolution (as it is called) and that of France are just the reverse of each other in almost every particular, and in the whole spirit of the transaction.'[40] Burke points out that the English had taken every care to preserve the constitution to which they were bound, stating, 'With us we got rid of the man, and preserved the constituent parts of the state. There they get rid of the constituent parts of the state, and keep the man.'[41] In short he believed that in 1688 England had been acting in accordance within the legal framework prescribed by the constitution; 'The Church and the State were the same after the Revolution that they were before, but better secured in every part.'[42]

In reference to Price's sermon, Burke writes that all rulers are obliged to follow the:

---

[38] Stanlis gives the most comprehensive description of the antithesis between will and reason as Burke perceived it. Peter J. Stanlis, *Edmund Burke and the Natural Law* (Lafayette: Huntington House, 1986), ch. 3.

[39] Edmund Burke 'Speech on the Army Estimates', *Works* Vol. V, p. 19.

[40] Ibid.

[41] Ibid., pp. 19-20.

[42] Ibid. p. 20.

steady maxims of faith, justice, and fixed fundamental policy, [which] are perfectly intelligible and perfectly binding upon those who exercise any authority, under any name or under any title, in the state. [43]

This intimates the first clue as to why it was so critical for Burke that the events of 1688 should be in accordance with constitutional law. He writes that it may be impossible to 'give limits to the mere *abstract* competence of the supreme power, such as was exercised by Parliament at that time', yet there were nevertheless 'the limits of a *moral* competence subjecting, even in powers more indisputably sovereign, occasional will to permanent reason'[44] which he found in the divine order. For Burke, working within the defined parameters of the constitution was a moral issue.[45] To flagrantly transgress the constitution was an assertion of will over the accumulated moral reason of centuries.

Burke's rejection of arbitrary will and the assertion of the natural law inhering within constitutional law was well established in the thought of the common lawyers and was a common characteristic of the pre-modern natural law tradition. As Merio Scattola points out, one of the defining features of pre-modern varieties of natural law discourse was a belief in a universal order of justice under which rulers were accountable. If they violated this order and ruptured the demands of justice then they were to be held accountable. Scatolla writes, 'Both the scholastic tradition of Thomas Aquinas and the Lutheranism of Melanchthon suppose the existence of a superior, universal order in which all existing rules play a role.' The consequence of this understanding of the natural law is that 'good and evil, virtue and vice, command and prohibition correspond

---

[43] Burke, *Reflections on the Revolution in France*, op. cit., p. 57.

[44] Ibid.

[45] The following statement from the House of Representatives perfectly encapsulates Burke's own view of the constitution, 'It is the glory of the British Prince and the happiness of all his subjects that their constitution hath its foundation in the immutable laws of nature; and as the supreme legislature, as well as the supreme executive derives its authority from that constitution, it should seem that no laws can be made or executed which are repugnant to any essential law of nature.' House of Reps. Of Mass. To Conway, [Feb. 13, 1768], Almon, *Prior Documents*, pp. 181-2. Quoted in Randolph Greenfield Adams, *Political Ideas of the American Revolution*, (New York: Barnes and Noble, 1939).

with an objective order that is given and cannot be changed'. On this account of justice, humans are aware of God's law predominantly through the natural law and the revelation of scripture. Importantly, this allows individuals to discern what constitutes just government. Consequently, 'The king who does not rule for the sake of his own subjects, but only seeks for his own private advantage, turns into a tyrant, who infringes the law of nature and will be punished both by men and by God.'[46]

How then does this relate to Rawls' liberalism? For conservatives, there are a number of beliefs espoused by Rawls that are misguided: the belief that we can deduce principles of justice by means of abstract reflection alone, the idea that we ought to select our constitutional essentials according to a (liberal) political conception of man, and the belief that this is the surest way to create a peace between opposing religious groups. As we have seen, Burke believed in a natural moral law, discernible by men and supplemented by the claims of the gospel. For Burke, this law demands justice, tolerance and mercy. But it is not a codified theocratic law. By virtue of our prudential judgements, it feeds into constitutional law, ensuring the preservation of justice. The greatest threat to justice was, in Burke's view, the unrestrained will of man. Whether Burke drew too close an association between the constitution and God's given order of justice is open to question. We can at least say, that in light of the democratically elected tyrants of the twentieth century, Burke's emphasis on the necessity for checks and balances on popular democracy and on the importance of an objective moral law, which feeds into constitutional law, seem justified. The *vox populi, vox dei*,[47] account of sovereignty has a poor history of preserving human dignity. For Burke, a society that aspired to orientate itself to the rights of man and placed an excessive focus on human autonomy risked recreating society in the image of a flawed humanity. He was swift to remind the world that neither regent nor commoner is ultimately sovereign:

All persons possessing any portion of power ought to be strongly

---

[46] Merio Scattola, 'Before and After Natural Law' in *Early Modern Natural Law Theories: Context and Strategies in the Early Enlightenment*, T.J. Hochstrasser and P. Shroeder (eds.), (Boston, Kluwer, 2003), p. 7.

[47] The phrase itself coming from an early eighteenth century radical Whig tract that denounced the existence of the natural law.

and awfully impressed with an idea that they act in trust; and that they are to account for their conduct in that trust to the one great Master, Author and Founder of society.

This principle ought even to be more strongly impressed upon the minds of those who compose the collective sovereignty, than upon those of single princes. [48]

This emphatic rejection of voluntarism which we find in Burke's reaction to Price was made on the basis that unrestrained human will inevitably leads to tyranny. In contrast to Rawls, Burke believed the surest way to preserve justice, peace and tolerance, was through the checks and balances of the institutions that had grown out of Britain's Christian culture. While a nation ultimately has the power to choose its own trajectory, Burke's emphasis on conservative, Christian oriented institutions encourages a society to mitigate the effects of ill-conceived, rapid change and retain its moral orientation from one generation to the next. In the next chapter I will look at the principles, rooted in doctrinal commitments, which form the basis of Burke's conservatism.

[48] Burke, *Reflections on the Revolution in France*, op. cit., pp. 177-178.

Chapter Six

The Six Theo-Political Principles of Burkean Conservatism

There can be no genuine conservatism which is not founded upon a religious view of the basis of civil obligation, and there can be no true religion where the basis of civil obligation is treated as purely secular.

This has been the conclusion of so many different Conservative thinkers that I should be utterly untrue to the Conservative tradition as well as to my own conviction were I not to say so.

Baron Hailsham, *The Case for Conservatism* (1947)

Up to this point we have brought the political thought of Edmund Burke into dialogue with the contractarian tradition. We have seen Burke offer a variety of arguments which seem to emerge from a body of political principles. In this chapter I highlight six practical political principles which can be identified in Edmund Burke's writings and in the political tradition which followed him. Although Burke did not articulate his political thought in overtly theological terms, Burke's political principles and his conservative approach to politics were based upon his understanding of the theology of the Christian faith.

Conservatism and Christianity
The term 'conservative' can be contentious, and some might say that to speak of the history of 'conservatism' is too ambiguous. Burke himself was a Whig and his admirers have included Whigs, Tories, utilitarians,

liberals and socialists. Furthermore, the tradition that is commonly identified as conservative is comprised of individuals with substantially divergent political views. The 'One Nation' conservatism of Disraeli was markedly different from the modernising and free market conservatism of Robert Peel and Lord Aberdeen. Furthermore, Christian Liberals such as Gladstone were deeply influenced by Burke and would have been sympathetic to most of the principles outlined in this chapter. Despite the potential ambiguity in speaking of 'Burkean conservatism', there is value in the term. I use the term 'Burkean' because Burke has articulated these principles more clearly than any other thinker and I use the term 'conservative' because these principles have chiefly been associated with the conservative tradition.

It is not a coincidence that the political principles which define conservatism resonate with many of the foundational assumptions of the Christian faith. Burke's Christian anthropology, eschatology and his belief in the natural law as a force of social formation were important influences on his politics. Similarly, notable conservatives who have followed Burke have also been heavily influenced in their political thought by their Christian faith. Lord Liverpool, Samuel Coleridge, Alexis de Tocqueville, George Canning, Robert Peel, Benjamin Disraeli, Lord Salisbury, Stanley Baldwin, T.S. Eliot, Christopher Dawson, Russell Kirk and Baron Hailsham: all of these held an approach to politics, which we might call conservative, on the basis of Christian convictions. In spite of the variety of these figures, the consonance between their political principles is not coincidental. The principles which undergird their political opinions are animated by predominantly Christian presuppositions and cannot be adequately explained without them.' This applies to the conservative critique of political liberalism. As Peter Stanlis writes, it was 'In the principles and history of Anglicanism, no less than in Catholicism, [that] Burke found much that opposed theories of primitive or "natural" society, much that nourished a system of civil manners which made possible the development of a free and just society.'[1]

---

[1] P. J. Stanlis, *Edmund Burke and the Natural Law*, op. cit., p. 204.

Conservatism as a set of political principles and not political ideology
All approaches to politics are vitalised by a tension between what is, and what ought to be, the case. In other words, there is an ethical consciousness at the heart of political discourse which pursues a perceived set of normative social goods. As such, from a Christian perspective, politics ought not to be conceived in purely secular terms but must always be a facet of the Christian ethical life. As William Temple wrote, 'If Christianity is true at all, it is a truth of universal application; all things should be done in the Christian spirit and in accordance with Christian principles.'[2]

The Christian gospel is charged with the tension between what is and what ought to be. For the Christian the 'ought' which drives an engagement with the world is not solely a product of reason or human imagination, but the received promise of a coming kingdom which has arrived in part but will one day reign in full. The crucial implication of this belief is that for Christians there can be no perfect political solution short of the *eschaton*, when the King himself will rule the kingdom and 'establish it with judgment and with justice henceforth even forever' (Isaiah 9:7 KJV). Until the advent of that new age all human polities will be marred by the sin and strife which are endemic to the world and the human condition. This belief is both religious and unavoidably political. In one breath it defies the claims of ideologies which promise salvation from our own fallenness and resulting limitations and insists upon the contingency and imperfectability of any political system. This is explained in Jesus' vivid Parable of the Tares in Matthew chapter 13. Until the coming of the Kingdom the wheat and the tares will grow side by side; good and evil will cohabit in the city of man. Political ideologies which do not begin with an admission of God's kingship are often marked by one commonality: a belief in the kingship of a secular system or ruler who can bring right order and enduring peace to the polity. In short, idolatry paves the road to ideology. If the Christian is to have any approach to politics at all, it cannot be an ideological one, because the vision of the coming Kingdom is neither for the labourers fully to know nor fully to consummate. If Christians are to engage in politics then they must be mindful of God as the architect of the coming Kingdom.

---

[2] William Temple, *Christianity and Social Order* (London: SCM Press, 1950), p. 48.

This means forfeiting pretensions to the divine mind and ultimately bowing the knee to the authority of God's rule in Christ. Practically, in the eschatological interim which we inhabit, this involves a refusal to accept political ideologies, especially those which hold out an illusory promise of enduring peace and true freedom aside from Christ. As Oliver O'Donovan writes, 'Just as there is only one true throne, so there is but one structured human community, and there can never be a second.'[3]

Burke's conservatism offers a *via media* between despairing pessimism at the possibility of any stable political project outside of Christ's final rule and the endeavour to instate an earthly utopia. Here we should draw a distinction between political principles and political ideology. Burke's conservatism, insofar as it is a political philosophy at all, is composed of principles. There is no grand political architecture which emerges from a set of axioms and climaxes in a prescriptive vision of how the polity ought to look. Fascism, communism and contractarian liberalism have all, at certain points in history, taken such an ideological form. Burke's conservatism offers no such universal vision.[4] In this regard, the conservative tradition has arguably been subject to a misnomer. There is clearly a degree of humility engendered by the conservative admission that in large part we are not architects but inheritors of all the good things we enjoy. Yet at the heart of Edmund Burke's understanding of social order is not simply conservation of the good things given to us by our forefathers, but the admission that God himself is the *Prima Causa* of the state, without whose authority it would be illegitimate.[5]

---

[3] Oliver O'Donovan, *The Desire of the Nations: Rediscovering the Roots of Political Theology* (Cambridge University Press, 1996), p. 156.

[4] In rejecting the idea that ethics and politics lay within the domain of speculative reason, Burke rejected the idea that a universally normative form of government or society could ever be deduced. Instead Burke believed that political forms and ethical questions were contingent upon circumstance.

[5] Burke made this point clearly on several occasions: 'All persons possessing any portion of power ought to be strongly and awfully impressed with an idea that that they act in trust; and that they are to account for their conduct in that trust to the one great master, author, and founder of society. This principle ought even to be more strongly impressed upon the minds of those who compose the collective sovereignties, than upon those of single princes'. Burke, *Reflections on the Revolution in France*, op. cit., pp. 177-178; 'We know and we feel inwardly that religion is the basis of civil society, and the source of all good and all comfort.' Burke, *Reflections on the Revolution in France*, op. cit., p. 173.

Conservation is then only one ancillary principle that emerges from the admission that we are not the authors of our own existence.

The idea that Christianity gives us principles and not a political model has been clearly articulated in Anglican social thought. In *Christianity and Social Order* William Temple wrote, 'There is no such thing as a Christian social ideal, to which we should conform our actual society as closely as possible... But though Christianity supplies no ideal in this sense, it supplies something of far more value – namely, principles on which we can begin to act in every possible situation.'[6] The Burkean tradition provides a body of such principles, by no means exhaustive, but nevertheless comprehensive, formulated primarily by Christians and indebted to their worldview. Burkean conservatism then is an integrated set of political principles, emerging from a Christian worldview to which the admission that God is sovereign is basic. These principles actively seek to establish right order within a specific context whilst resisting any prescriptive political vision precisely because of the admission that God is sovereign.

One criticism of conservatism is that it offers no social vision, no universally normative account of what a society ought to look like. It is said that it merely affirms an arbitrary status quo and petulantly resists the tides of change. This criticism is entirely valid if conservatism is severed from its Christian moorings. Conservatism is a broad church and there are conservatives who simply articulate a belief in maintaining social stability by resisting change, David Hume being the forefather of this line of conservatism. This is not Burkean conservatism. For the Christian, Burke offers no grand political framework and therefore allows a religious vision to occupy the heart of the political endeavour. This means that particular ethical issues, whether concerning the nature of life, the family or concern for the underprivileged, can be pursued from a Christian perspective within a political system without destroying it.

This conservatism does not favour a theocracy precisely because it limits itself to a body of political principles which are based upon the Christian faith but also emerge from a Christian's engagement with politics. By contrast, a theocracy would seek to institute a comprehensive political vision, bringing the divine into the contingent. A Christian

---

[6] William Temple, *Christianity and Social Order* op.cit., p. 52.

eschatology defies the belief that God's consummated rule could ever be reduced to a political formula which weds the *New Jerusalem* to *Babylon*. In Burke's thinking, it is because God's final rule will exceed the transience of the present age that theocracy cannot be an alternative for Christians.

T.S. Eliot agreed, writing that 'to identify any particular form of government with Christianity is a dangerous error: for it confounds the permanent with the transitory, the absolute with the contingent'.[7] At the heart of the conceptual consonance between Burkean conservatism and Christianity lies Burke's refusal to offer a political architecture which will right the wrongs of the world. The distinction between principles and ideal political systems was one which Burke himself made clear: 'When I praised the British constitution and wished it to be well studied, I did not mean that its exterior form and positive arrangement should become a model for you, or for any people serviley to copy. I meant to recommend the principles from which it has grown, and the policy on which it has been progressively improved out of elements common to you and to us'.[8] In a similar passage he wrote: 'without the guide and light of sound, well-understood principles, all reasonings in politics, as in everything else, would be only a confused jumble of particular facts and details, without the means of drawing out any sort of theoretical or practical conclusion'.[9]

Burke's conservatism finds principles preferable to a substantive vision of an ideal political arrangement because Christians already have a conception of Heaven and this is not on earth. Conservative thinkers have advocated conservation in the conviction that we inhabit an interim. As a result they did not strive for the eschatological fulfilment of all things, but instead adopted an attitude of caution, aspiring to preserve just institutions, truth and right judgement where they found it. Burke did not resist the involvement of religious feeling in politics, but actively resisted any attempt to institute Heaven on earth. To the pragmatist who would say that conservatism ought to favour these principles not

[7] T. S. Eliot, *The Idea of a Christian Society* (New York, NY: Harcourt, Brace, 1939), p. 57.
[8] Burke, 'Letter to a Member of the National Assembly', *The Works,* op. cit., Vol. VI, p. 57-58.
[9] Burke, 'Speech on the Petition of the Unitarians', *The Works,* op. cit., Vol. X, p. 41.

because of their Christian roots but because they work, the Burkean conservative might reply that they work because they are attuned to the true realities of the world which are explained by the Christian faith. To this principle we now turn.

Principle 1. *Reckoning with reality*

In the 1960s the United States found its historically Christian culture challenged both internally and externally by communism and socialism. In opposition to this challenge there arose a conservative outcry. Russell Kirk was perhaps the chief herald of the distinction between ideological dogma and conservative principle. Kirk wrote that 'the attitude we call conservatism is sustained by a body of sentiments, rather than by a system of ideological dogmata'.[10]

In Burke's critique of the liberalism in his own day we can see a sustained attack upon what he believed to be an element of fantasy in the thought of contractarian thinkers: from the state of nature, to natural rights and a political framework. Burke's exasperation was centred on the fact that if such doctrines do not correspond to reality then, instead of heaven on earth, the liberal society would risk declining into hell on earth, no matter how benign the revolutionaries' intentions. He wrote: 'A man full of warm, speculative benevolence may wish his society otherwise constituted than he finds it, but a good patriot and a true politician always considers how he shall make the most of the existing materials of his country.'[11] It was Burke's political realism which grounded his belief in the necessity of stable and legitimate governance. Burke's affinity with the common law tradition is no coincidence; as Roger Scruton notes: 'Law is constrained at every point by reality, and utopian visions have no place in it. Moreover the common law of England is proof that there is a real distinction between legitimate and illegitimate power, that power can exist without oppression, and that authority is a living force in human conduct'.[12]

As we have seen, Burke's political realism, which emerged from

---

[10] Russell Kirk, 'Ten Conservative Principles', http://www.kirkcenter.org/index.php/detail/ten-conservative-principles/, (accessed 22nd October 2013).

[11] Burke, *Reflections on the Revolution in France,* op. cit., p. 285.

[12] Roger Scruton 'Why I Became a Conservative', in *The New Criterion*, 21 (Feb. 2003), p. 4.

a Christian inheritance rooted in Thomism and Aristotelian realism, brought him into opposition with the liberal doctrines which he perceived served as the justification for the revolutionaries' voluntaristic approach to politics. As Joseph Pappin III writes, 'I hold that it is irrefutable that Burke's politics adheres to a natural law foundation which permeates his thinking'. It was 'the off-spring of his theistic stance' and it grounds his 'realist understanding of human nature'.[13]

The realism which coincided with Burke's theological view of human nature and the physical and spiritual world provided the basis for a gritty engagement with reality, in which the necessity for bulwarking oneself against the fact of human evil is readily apparent. C.S. Lewis famously wrote that 'I believe in Christianity as I believe that the sun has risen: not only because I see it, but because by it I see everything else'.[14] A Christian worldview has framed the political discourse of many in the conservative tradition. From a Christian perspective, this has enabled them to see reality with a more acute focus.

As we have seen, Burke held a belief in the illuminating nature of the Christian faith and it undergirded his conviction that all men, particularly those of any great influence, should consider themselves to have a religious vocation. William Temple writes: 'Christians have some clues to the understanding of human nature which may enable them to make a more accurate estimate than others of these points. But they will not, if they are true to their own tradition, approach the question with rosy-tinted spectacles. Its assertion of original sin should make the Church intensely realistic, and conspicuously free from Utopianism.'[15] To this principle we turn.

Principle 2. *Human fallenness, Human limitation and Human Sociality*
One characteristic which is closely aligned with the epistemic realism inherent in Burke's thought is a political realism as to the nature of uncivilised man. For the Christian this is the most basic of doctrines at the heart of the Christian faith. In all areas of life Christians must reckon

---

[13] Joseph Pappin III, 'Edmund Burke's Progeny: Recent Scholarship on Burke's Political Philosophy', *Political Science Reviewer*, 35 (2006), p. 14.

[14] C.S Lewis, 'Is Theology Poetry?' in *The Weight of Glory: And Other Addresses* (New York, NY: 1949, HarperCollins), p. 140.

[15] Temple, *Christianity and Social Order,* op. cit., p. 51.

with the fallenness of man and the consequences which will arise if man's sinful nature is left utterly autonomous and unchecked. As it is articulated in the Thirty Nine Articles, 'it is the fault and corruption of the Nature of every man, that naturally is ingendered [sic] of the offspring of Adam; whereby man is very far gone from original righteousness, and is of his own nature inclined to evil, so that the flesh lusteth always contrary to the spirit'. Divorced from this most basic admission, the Mosaic Law, the incarnation, the resurrection, the Church and the eschatological renewal are all rendered incomprehensible. The contractarian tradition refuses the image of Adam shamed and banished from Eden, and shuns the image of Cain, standing bloodied over his lifeless brother. Temple makes the point well: 'the political problem is concerned with men as they are, not with men as they ought to be. Part of the task is so to order life as to lead them nearer to what they ought to be; but to assume that they are already this will involve in certain failure and disaster'.[16]

Temple's voice is aligned with that of Burke's two hundred years after Burke's assessment of liberalism's basic doctrines, which he believed to be dangerously optimistic about the reality of man's nature in an uncivilised world devoid of the rule of law. Burke lamented that the revolutionaries 'systematically corrupt a very corruptible race'.[17] His view of man was characterised by an optimism about the place of man in God's original creation and the capacity for man to do good should he be governed properly, but a profound sobriety regarding the nature of man ungoverned and loosed from all chains of social restraint.

The Christian doctrine of man offers an anthropology which rejects that offered by the contractarian tradition. First, the Christian doctrine of man begins at a temporal point with man as a created being affirmed by God (Genesis 2). It is in God's affirmation that man is defined and his relations with others are defined (1 John 4:19). O'Donovan writes:

sociality itself is not a bare empirical *datum*, but a historical and eschatological destiny. It is something we cannot pretend to get behind, as though there were a pre-social individual human nature with 'basic needs' that generated society as an instrument for its own protection. When God said 'it is not good for man to be alone', that

---

[16] Temple, *Christianity and Social Order,* op. cit., p. 50.
[17] Burke, 'Letter to a Member of the National Assembly', p. 36.

was not an afterthought, but the determining moment in the creation of the human race.[18]

We shall turn shortly to the conservative understanding of man's natural affections and prejudices, but for now we can note that Burke was clear that man is naturally a social being, always and already in community with those around him, conditioned by those who have come before him and ultimately in relation with his divine maker. Because of this conviction, one of Burke's main criticisms of what he called the 'Synagogue of Antichrist' (by which he meant 'the sect which predominated in the Constituent Assembly of 1789') was that 'All their new institutions (and with them everything is new) strike at the root of our social nature'.[19] Such an understanding of the sociality of man ran deep in his intellectual bloodline from Cicero, Hooker and the Anglican divines to Coke and Blackstone. The sociality of man finds its most comprehensive articulation in Burke's redefinition of the social contract and it underlies his convictions concerning the civil tissue which binds the social body together. Burke's engagement with politics was mindful of the human person as an already relational being, dependent from her very conception, endowed with duties by her creator and always ontologically dependent upon another – a more complicated conception of the human condition than that of the contractarian tradition.

The Burke scholar Niemeyer cites the inherent sociality of man as one reason that we cannot 'fall back on Locke's human rights, the condition on which each isolated person enters human community by the gate of *quid pro quo*. These and other similar worldviews have nothing to say to the reality of living human beings with body and soul, mind and spirit'.[20] While, at points, Locke did stress the importance of particular civic duties, Niemeyer rightly points towards the 'social contract' to illustrate an atomism in Locke's conception of society. The Christian belief that humans were from their conception social and dependent beings militates against the liberal reductionism which

[18] Oliver O'Donovan, *The Ways of Judgement* (Cambridge: Eerdmans, 2005), p. 241.
[19] Edmund Burke, 'Letters on a Regicide Peace', *The Works*, op. cit., Vol. XIII, p. 173-174.
[20] Gerhart Niemeyer, 'Russell Kirk and Ideology', *The InterCollegiate Review*, Vol. 30 (Fall, 1994), pp. 35-38.

draws conclusions about the normative form of society from the alleged character of the pre-social individuals who compose the whole. Ramsay comments that liberal theories of society 'are reductionist in that they assert that the compositional units of the whole are ontologically [and chronologically] prior to the whole'.[21] As a result, the polity proposed by the contractarians of Burke's day was a society which, Burke believed, had an excessive esteem for autonomy, denying the need for dependence and ultimately magnifying the aberrant excesses of man's fallen nature instead of curbing them.

Burke argued that it was because of human vanity that the revolutionaries enthroned the individual. Speaking of Rousseau's influence he wrote 'under this philosophic instructor in the ethics of vanity, they have attempted in France a regeneration of the moral constitution of man'[22] and, as a result, the revolutionaries revelled in 'absurd theory'.[23] In Burke's estimation such individualism would ultimately bear toxic fruit: 'the commonwealth itself would, in a few generations, crumble away, be disconnected into the dust and powder of individuality, and at length dispersed to all the winds of heaven'.[24]

Burke's anthropology is more closely aligned to the Christian doctrine of man than the Lockean man in the state of nature. Burke wrote of the revolutionaries: 'This sort of people are so taken up with their theories about the *Rights* of man, that they have totally forgotten his *nature*.'[25] Conservatives such as Russell Kirk have argued that the corroding power of sin is indifferent to the hypothetical distinctions between public and private. If sin is deemed acceptable and even encouraged in our private lives then, like a virus, it will inevitably pervade the public life of the polity. As an approach to politics which embraces reality at its most acute, conservatives from Burke to Kirk have articulated an account of man as a fallen yet an inherently social, created being. As the Burke scholar Richard Hoff wrote: 'The most important questions about the

[21] Maureen Ramsay, *What's Wrong With Liberalism? A Radical Critique of Liberal Political Philosophy*, op. cit., p. 8.
[22] Burke, 'Letter to a member of the National Assembly', *The Works*, op. cit., Vol. VI, p. 36.
[23] Ibid., p. 3.
[24] Burke, *Reflections on the Revolution in France,* op. cit., p. 183.
[25] Burke, 'Letter to a member of the National Assembly', *The Works*, op. cit., Vol. VI, p. 130.

human race Burke answered from the Church of England's catechism'.[26]

Principle 3. *A refusal of ideological claims*

We have already noted that, if Christians are to be true to the gospel proclamation of Christ's lordship, then they cannot accept political ideology because the absolute cannot be assimilated to the contingent. An acknowledgment of God's kingship and the new order of creation held together in Christ defies the absolute pretensions of temporal authorities and demands that their judgments are subordinated to God's if they are to be legitimate. In this sense ideology does not hold that 'Jesus is Lord', instead proclaiming the lordship of another – in the case of Bolshevik communism, economic equality, and in the case of Nazi fascism, the nation state. In its worst form, contractarian liberalism has enthroned a conception of the autonomous man. In what Burke referred to as a form of 'political geometry', ideologies of all stripes draw a blueprint of the polity in accordance with a governing first principle. In attempting to re-order society towards a distinctive teleology, other social goods become disordered and the fabric of the nation is torn apart. As O'Donovan puts it: 'A social order based on a single principle, however fine, becomes ideological; and a political theology which defends freedom without filling it out with the content of the divine command and the divine redemption of society in Christ is ideologically liberal'.[27]

Rather than men being stewards in the creative project, ideologies assert a political architecture upon which the labourers are so transfixed that they are blind and deaf to God's active voice in the polity. In Matthew's gospel, Christians are admonished to be ever vigilant against false prophets who come with messianic pretensions (Matthew 24: 3-8). During the twentieth century the church has been acutely aware of the threat of ideology. In 1891 Pope Leo XIII penned *Rerum Novarum* in which he condemned the materialism of free market liberalism as well as the ideologies of communism and socialism. In 1931 Pope Pius XI argued in *Quadragesimo Anno* that communism and socialism in all their forms could find no truce with the Christian religion precisely

---

[26] Ross Hoffman and Paul Levack, *Burke's Politics* (New York, NY: Alfred A. Knopf, 1949), p. xiv.
[27] Oliver O'Donovan, *The Desire of the Nations, Rediscovering the Roots of Political Theology* (Cambridge University Press, 1996), p. 250.

because they idolised the material means of production and excluded the gospel. He wrote: 'let all remember that liberalism is the father of this Socialism that is pervading morality and culture and that Bolshevism will be its heir'.[28] This is a critique that was strongly supported in *Mater et Magistra* by Pope John XXIII. More recently, Pope Benedict XVI issued *Caritas in Veritate* in which he warned against 'merely human' utopian and ideological visions posed by technology and a blind faith in the free market.[29]

Protestants have been no less alive to the threat. In Karl Barth's 1934 'Theological Declaration of Barmen' he made the point that ideologies of all stripes must be considered pretenders to the throne of Christ and must be rejected by Christians, whose vocation is to preach the gospel, not least to the state. As Russell Kirk pointed out: 'Ideology is inverted religion' which operates by 'denying the Christian doctrine of salvation through grace in death' instead holding the illusory promise of 'salvation here on earth'.[30] The reality of God's sovereignty conflicts with all ideological claims which is why Karl Rahner defined ideology as 'an erroneous system which must be rejected by a true interpretation of reality'.[31]

The conservative tradition has, at its roots, a scepticism of totalising ideologies and a deep respect for creative human freedom in civil society. This lack of comprehensive political vision preserves a sanctified space for the joint operation of God and man, one site of which is in man's prayerful prudence. O'Donovan writes: 'God builds God's kingdom. But God has ordered his world in such a way that his own work would take place not least through one of his creatures in particular, namely the human beings who reflect his image... He has enlisted us to act as

---

[28] Pope Pius IX, *Quadragesimo Anno* [Encylical Letter on Reconstruction of the Social Order], §122, http://w2.vatican.va/content/pius-xi/en/encyclicals/documents/hf_p-xi_enc_19310515_quadragesimo-anno.html, (accessed 21st January, 2015).

[29] Pope Benedict XVI, *Caritas In Veritate* [Encyclical Letter on Integral Human Development in Charity and Truth], §53, http://w2.vatican.va/content/benedict-xvi/en/encyclicals/documents/hf_ben-xvi_enc_20090629_caritas-in-veritate.html, (accessed 21st January, 2015).

[30] Kirk, 'Ten Conservative Principles', op. cit., p. 4.

[31] Karl Rahner, 'Ideology and Christianity', *Theological Investigations*, trans. Karl-H. and Boniface Krueger (Baltimore: Helicon, 1969), Vol. VI, 43-58.

his stewards in the project of creation.'[32] It is for this reason that the Christian must reject an ideal form of government in favour of a system of government that seeks to conform itself to God's law. As Pope Leo XIII wrote: 'by the State we here understand, not the particular form of government prevailing in this or that nation, but the State as rightly apprehended; that is to say, any government conformable in its institutions to right reason and natural law'.[33]

Burke reminds us that a healthy society consists in the gradual accumulation of a body of law which nurtures society as an organism, to embody the ends ordained by its creator. For Burke, the Christian gospel is central to this task by providing a personal ethical code that shapes the customs and manners of society. He believed that religion was closely associated with the 'observance of law and order' and 'honest industry'.[34] Burke rejected the suggestion that the complex web of human life, replete with myriad social goods which often operate in symphony, could be reduced to one governing first axiom. The one first axiom which might justifiably cite at the heart of Burke's work is that of God's sovereignty. However, a foundational belief in the sovereignty of a relational God cannot be converted into a political system. To assert God's sovereignty is to defer to the untameable, ineffable and incomprehensible mystery of God's own being. Moreover, it is to accept that his ways are unfathomable and his thoughts untraceable. The admission that God alone is rightfully the founder, sustainer and guide of society encourages a radically different approach to our political endeavours. No longer are we political architects drawing a blueprint for the polity, but we are labourers attentive to the director's voice in each concrete circumstance by means of prayerful prudence.

In such a picture, the movement is from God to man, not man to God. The gospel narrative relates how man was unable to attain his own salvation by his own works, but instead the absolute deity plunged into the particular and in Jesus met man in a set of concrete circumstances. So in their approach to politics Christians should reject any attempt to attain

---

[32] Oliver O'Donovan, The *Desire of the Nations*, op. cit., p. 218.

[33] Pope Leo XIII, *Rerum Novarum*, Encyclical Letter on Capital and Labour, §32, http://w2.vatican.va/content/leo-xiii/en/encyclicals/documents/hf_l-xiii_enc_15051891_rerum-novarum.html, (accessed 21st January, 2015).

[34] Burke, 'An Abridgement of the English History', *The Works*, op. cit., Vol. X, p. 293.

their own salvation, which has already been attained, instead remaining attentive to the word of God who meets them in their particular needs and helps them in the (sometimes political) challenges that they face. As Burke put it: 'can it be imagined... that He will suffer this great gift of government, the greatest, the best, that was ever given by God to mankind, to be the plaything and the sport of the feeble will of a man, who, by a blasphemous, absurd, and petulant usurpation would place his own feeble, contemptible, ridiculous will in the place of Divine wisdom and Justice?'.[35]

Burke favoured cautious prudence rather than an abstract rule: 'To enable us to correct the Constitution, the whole Constitution must be viewed together; and it must be compared with the actual state of the people, and the circumstances of the time... Please God, I will walk with caution, whenever I am not able clearly to see my way before me.'[36] Speaking of the Christian religion as the cornerstone of the English system of government, Burke wrote: 'The body of all true religion consists, to be sure, in obedience to the will of the Sovereign of the world, in a confidence in his declarations, and in imitation of his perfections.'[37] Burke is quite clear that the enthronement of enlightenment reason was no substitute for the guiding light of wisdom, 'Dr. Price seems rather to over value the great acquisitions of light which he has obtained and diffused in this age'.[38] In Burke's view, it was a misplaced faith in man's reason which caused the revolutionaries to 'march from error to error, through a dry desert, unguided by the lights of heaven, or by the contrivance which wisdom has invented to supply their place'. Burke intimated that in turning away from the 'lights of heaven', the vainglorious ideology of the revolutionaries followed in the footsteps of Satan's own self apotheosis:

They endeavour to destroy that tribunal of conscience which exists

---

[35] Burke, 'Speech in the Impeachment of Warren Hastings', *The Works*, op. cit., Vol. XIII, p. 66-167.
[36] Edmund Burke, 'A Letter to the Chairman of the Buckinghamshire Meeting, Held at Aylesbury, April 13, 1780 on the Subject of Parliamentary Reform' in *The Best of Burke: Selected Writings and Speeches of Edmund Burke* (Washington D.C.: Regnery, 1963), pp. 383-384.
[37] Burke, *Reflections on the Revolution in France*, op. cit., p. 289.
[38] Ibid., p. 132.

independently of edicts and decrees. Your despots govern by terror.
They know that he who fears God fears nothing else; and therefore
they eradicate from the mind, through their Voltaire, their Helvetius,
and the rest of that infamous gang, that only sort of fear which
generates true courage. Their object is, that their fellow citizens
may be under the dominion of no awe, but that of their committee
of research, and of their lanterne.[39]

If Burkean conservatism upholds God's sovereignty, it is no coincidence
that his political thought seems at times unsystematic and even
inconsistent. Burke believed that the statesman's thought ought to be
regulated by a prudence ever conscious of God's sovereignty in complex
concrete circumstances. He made this point in his *Speech to the Electors
of Bristol*, in which he defined the role of a statesman: 'His enlightened
conscience, he ought not to sacrifice to you; to any man, or to any set of
men living. These he does not derive from your pleasure; no nor from the
Law and the Constitution. They are a trust from Providence, for the abuse
of which he is deeply answerable.'[40] His contractarian adversaries had by
contrast, in his view, no qualms in sacrificing prudential considerations at
the altar of a governing first principle. Burke knew that in idolising their
philosophy the revolutionaries sought to abolish the Christian religion:
'They who will not believe that the philosophical fanatics who guide
in these matters entertain a design of utterly abolishing the Christian
religion... are utterly ignorant of its character and proceedings.'[41]

Burke perceived that from God's sovereignty follows the right order
of the nation, political and civil. He paints a graphic picture of what
happens when a nation turns its back on God in favour of human reason:

I call it *Atheism by Establishment,* when any State, as such, shall
not acknowledge the existence of God as a moral Governor of the
World; when it shall offer to Him no religious or moral worship:
when it shall abolish the Christian religion by a regular decree;

---

[39] Burke, 'Letter to a Member of the National Assembly', *The Works*, op. cit., Vol. VI,
p. 41.
[40] Burke, 'Speech at Mr. Burke's Arrival at Bristol, and at the Conclusion of the Poll',
The Works, op. cit., Vol. III, pp. 18-19.
[41] Burke, *Reflections on the Revolution in France*, op. cit., p. 270.

when it shall persecute with a cold, unrelenting, steady cruelty, by every mode of confiscation, imprisonment, exile, and death, all its ministers; when it shall generally shut up, or pull down, churches; when the few buildings which remain of this kind shall be opened only for the purpose of making a profane apotheosis of monsters whose vices and crimes have no parallel amongst men, and whom all other men consider as objects of general detestation, and the severest animadversion of law. When, in the place of that religion of social benevolence, and of individual self-denial, in mockery of all religion, they institute impious, blasphemous, indecent theatric rites, in honour of their vitiated, perverted reason, and erect altars to the personification of their own corrupted and bloody Republic; when schools and seminaries are founded at public expense to poison mankind, from generation to generation, with the horrible maxims of this impiety; when wearied out with incessant martyrdom, and the cries of a people hungering and thirsting for religion, they permit it, only as a tolerated evil — I call this *Atheism by Establishment*.[42]

As well as seeing the dangers of atheism, Burke also understood the importance of Christianity as an active social force civilising the customs and manners of a society.

For some, the idea that the Christian God's sovereignty is the precondition for healthy political discourse implies intolerance; as Temple points out, 'no one really wants to live in the ideal state as depicted by anyone else'.[43] But Temple identifies an important point. We have seen that Christians should be wary of the notion that we are able to discover a universal model for an 'ideal' state. But there is a positive here as well. In the absence of an ideal political architecture, conservatism preserves a space for debate, plural voices and mutual enrichment in the construction of the polity; but, crucially, the necessary prerequisite for that space of communication is a cultural admission that God is sovereign. As Nigel Biggar points out 'there can be no such thing as a public order that is morally, anthropologically and metaphysically neutral. It must commit itself one way or another'. It is therefore

---

[42] Burke, 'Letters on a Regicide Peace', *The Works*, op. cit., Vol. XIII, pp. 170-171.
[43] Temple, *Christianity and Social Order*, op. cit., p. 52.

'inevitable that some members of a plural society will find themselves in a public order that affirms a worldview that is more or less different to their own'.[44]

Following Aquinas, we might argue that only God as God can so transcend our understanding that he defies any univocal conception or appropriation as an idol. Therefore it is only when God is our final end that our lives and our political discourse are perceived correctly.[45] Without such an admission, the space for toleration and mutual enrichment, insisted upon by Christian conservatives such as Burke and Disraeli, risks being usurped by an ideological vision. As Chesterton is said to have pointed out, there is no such thing as a vacuum of belief; 'when a man stops believing in God he doesn't then believe in nothing, he believes anything'. Burke made the same point when he remonstrated against those who believed 'we should uncover our nakedness by throwing off that Christian religion which has hitherto been our boast and comfort, and one great source of civilization amongst us'. He proceeded to write 'that the mind will not endure a void' and should the nation lose its Christian faith 'some uncouth, pernicious, and degrading superstition might take place of it.'[46]

Principle 4. *Authority and freedom*

If Burke's realism was premised on a rationally intelligible, divinely ordained order, so was his understanding of authority. An acceptance of authority, be it divine, political, civil or customary, is another principle of conservatism deeply indebted to the influence of Christianity. As we have seen, Burke's understanding of an intelligible world created by a God, whose intellect and will were in perfect harmony, led him to defend a hierarchically ordered universe, forthrightly rejecting the voluntarist notion of the legitimacy of rulers who governed by pure will. Peter Stanlis writes that because Burke believed that all authority was from God 'it was imperative, therefore, that all men, and particularly rulers,

---

[44] Nigel Biggar, *Between Kin and Cosmopolis: An Ethic of the Nation* (Eugene, OR: Cascade, 2014), p. 45.

[45] Thomas Aquinas, *Summa Theologica: Prima Parta*, trans. Fathers of the English Dominican Province, 1920, found at http://www.newadvent.org/summa/index.html (accessed 11th March 2014), Q. 13, A. 10.

[46] Burke, *Reflections on the Revolution in France*, op. cit., p. 174.

should "acknowledge the existence of God as a moral governor of the world"'.[47] It was this conviction that led Burke to write of the Christian religion that 'we will have her to exalt her mitred front in courts and parliaments. We will have her mixed throughout the whole mass of life and blended with all the classes of society'.[48] It seems likely that he would have approved of William Temple's sentiment that 'All Christian thinking, and Christian thinking about society no less than any other, must begin not with man but with God.'[49]

The hierarchy of authority, emanating from the divine and apportioned to individuals in office as representatives of the people is well summarised in the following passage taken from the *Reflections*. Burke's arguments show that he was profoundly concerned that those who wield power should be deeply conscious of the source of their power and to whom they are ultimately accountable. And he clearly articulates the illegitimacy of rulers who do not subject themselves to the natural law:

When the people have emptied themselves of all the lust of selfish will, which without religion it is utterly impossible they ever should, when they are conscious that they exercise, and exercise perhaps in a higher link of the order of delegation, the power, which to be legitimate must be according to that eternal, immutable law in which will and reason are the same, they will be more careful how they place power in base and incapable hands. In their nomination to office, they will not appoint to the exercise of authority as to a pitiful job, but as to a holy function, not according to their sordid, selfish interest, nor to their wanton caprice, nor to their arbitrary will, but they will confer that power (which any man may well tremble to give or to receive) on those only in whom they may discern that predominant proportion of active virtue and wisdom, taken together and fitted to the charge, such as in the great and inevitable mixed mass of human imperfections and infirmities is to be found.[50]

The exercise of authority being described as a holy function which should be received in fear and trembling is particularly striking. For

[47] Stanlis, *Edmund Burke and the Natural Law,* op. cit., p. 205.
[48] Burke, *Reflections on the Revolution in France*, op. cit., p. 197.
[49] Temple, *Christianity and Social Order*, op. cit., p. 52.
[50] Burke, *Reflections on the Revolution in France*, op. cit., p. 180.

Burke, political power is always conceived of as the vicarious exercise of divine power. Acutely aware of the 'mass of human imperfections and infirmities', Burke commends individuals of 'active virtue and wisdom' in order that society may be ordered rightly under their prudential judgements in accordance with the 'immutable law'. For conservatives since Burke, defending the cultural primacy and the political establishment of the Christian faith has allowed legitimate political claims to be made regarding the authoritative created moral order in which any society exists. This inevitably impacts upon the way a nation is governed and the customs and manners which citizens cultivate: from the effect it has upon a legislator's understanding of the right ends of human nature, to the way it affects citizens' judgements of particular moral claims. A society which accepts the establishment of the Christian faith is free in its public discourse to overtly acknowledge a world that is animated by moral forces and ordered by a creator.

The conservative emphasis on institutional authority is paradoxically inspired by a deep concern for the preservation of freedom. Winston Churchill captured this apparent paradox in Burke's thought well when he wrote, 'on the one hand he is revealed as a foremost apostle of Liberty, on the other as the redoubtable champion of Authority'. Churchill drew the correct conclusion when he wrote 'No one can read the Burke of Liberty and the Burke of Authority without feeling that here was the same man pursuing the same ends, seeking the same ideals of society and Government.'[51] The species of freedom of which Burke spoke is the freedom which is only found in the exercise of one's duty in communion with others. Since duty implies authority, the two operate in unison and are paramount to Burke's thought. Again, this emerged from a Christian anthropology which rejects the exercise of unrestrained will in the belief that true freedom was to be found under the divine law and within a community conceived by God. This understanding of freedom under the law was present in all of Burke's major influences, from Cicero to the common lawyers and, indirectly, through Aquinas and Aristotle. In the face of a radical redefinition of freedom, Burke harked back to the pre-modern conception of freedom inspired by conformity to law. A

---

[51] Winston Churchill, 'Consistency in Politics' (1932) in James W. Muller (ed.) *Thoughts and Adventures: Churchill Reflects on Spies, Cartoons, Flying and the Future* (Wilmington, DE: ISI, 2009), p. 40.

contemporary conservative rendering of the dynamic between authority and freedom is offered by Roger Scruton who captures the freedom found in the common law:

> Liberal thinkers... have seen the constraints on freedom as arising only negatively and in response to individual rights. Freedom should be qualified only by the possibility that someone might suffer through its exercise. For the conservative constraint should be upheld, until it can be shown that society is not damaged by its removal. Thus the constraints on freedom arise through the law's attempts to embody (as for a conservative it must embody) the fundamental values of the society which it aims to rule.[52]

It is out of the creative freedom bestowed by the acknowledgement of God's sovereignty that customs, traditions and institutions will flourish.

Principle 5. *An emphasis on customs, traditions and institutions*
The conservative emphasis on customs (often embodied in law), traditions and institutions is deeply attuned to the principles we have already noted, namely a belief in the creatureliness of man, a rejection of abstract ideology and a belief in the authority of the natural law which brings right order to a polity through prudential judgements. The historical point of convergence between Christianity and this aspect of conservatism is in the common lawyers and originally Thomas Aquinas. In this sense, Burke's conservatism is more aligned with the Thomistic tradition than the Augustinian. Burke's conservatism seems to be less well captured by Augustine's doctrine of the two cities than it is by Aquinas' polity of divinely ordained natural ends in which the good is realised in community with others. Michael Banner articulates Aquinas' political thought:

> For the Thomist tradition, which thinks of society as existing outside the church in virtue of the claims made upon human life by its natural ends, it is the common good that serves to unite its parts. The classical organic image of society thus maintains its naturalistic quality, with a special emphasis, however, on the need for the head

---

[52] Roger Scruton, *The Meaning of Conservatism* (Basingstoke: Palgrave, 2001), p. 15.

to identify the common good and coordinate its pursuit.[53]

This image of the social body directed towards the common good by a political head is one which was employed by Aristotle and Cicero before Aquinas. After Aquinas, John of Salisbury and common lawyers such as Fortescue and Blackstone employed the same metaphor. The metaphor resonates with Burke's thought. Yet, it is important to note that Burke's understanding of the polity was not authoritarian, ordering society from the top down. Rather, because the government was directed by right judgements, it was able to reflect the constitution of the body of which it was a natural extension. Defending the integrity of the particular character of individual societies and embracing this difference as part of God's created order are aspirations which have a natural place in the conservative tradition. It is a principle which finds strong biblical precedent. The story of the tower of Babel militates against a belief in the univocal reason of humanity, enabling people corporately to ascend the heights of heaven by virtue of their own will. It is a story that is opposed to any belief in the efficacy of a universal reason to construct the polity without conceding Christ's sovereignty.

Aquinas' thought has less rupture than Augustine's between the pre-lapsarian (before the fall) order and the post-lapsarian. For example, Aquinas sees man as naturally social and political and does not therefore regard political power as a necessary evil. One commentator put it well:

Under Aristotelian influence St. Thomas exchanged the Augustinian conception of a conflictual and disjunctive social order for a more organically harmonious one. His minimising of the spiritual distance between the traditionally 'pre-lapsarian' institutions such as marriage and family and the post-lapsarian institutions such as private property and political rule enabled him to weave social life into a unified moral texture. He viewed sinful society as retaining the inherent harmony of a hierarchy of natural ends and functions, each part having its appointed place within the teleological whole. With no disjunctive division between different communities, especially between political and non-political communities, all together constituted a real social

---

[53] Michael Banner, 'Christianity and Civil Society', in *Christian Political Ethics*, John A. Coleman, ed., (Princeton, NJ: Princeton University Press, 2007), p. 9.

totality, a common will directed toward a common good.[54]

Burke shared this organic vision of society. In Burke's thought, the civil and the political were not distinct but two interpenetrating spheres. Political society and the laws of the nation emerge from the accumulated customs of the people and naturally reflect them.

Burke's description of customary manners conveys well the bottom-up formation of society; laws are derived from manners and customs, not the other way round:

> Manners are of more importance than laws. Upon them, in a great measure, the laws depend. The law touches us but here and there, and now and then. Manners are what vex or sooth, corrupt or purify, exalt or debase, barbarize or refine us, by a constant, steady, uniform, insensible operation, like that of the air we breathe in. They give their whole form and colour to our lives. According to their quality, they aid morals, they supply them, or they totally destroy them.[55]

Equally important are customs, described as:

> obligations written in the heart. They approximate men to men, without their knowledge, and sometimes against their intentions. The secret, unseen, but irrefragable bond of habitual intercourse, holds them together, even when their perverse and litigious nature sets them to equivocate, scuffle, and fight about the terms of their written obligations.[56]

An emphasis on custom has a long heritage in Christian thought. As Aquinas wrote: 'custom has the force of law, and abolishes a law, and is the interpreter of laws.' He is careful, however, to note that 'no custom can acquire the force of law against divine or natural law', but must be subordinate to both.[57]

Aside from the Thomistic heritage of the idea, the conservative emphasis on customs and traditions seems to resonate deeply with the

[54] Joan O'Donovan, quoted in Banner, 'Christianity and Civil Society', op. cit., p. 9.
[55] Burke, 'Letters on a Regicide Peace', *The Works, op. cit.*, Vol. XIII, p. 172.
[56] Ibid., p. 181.
[57] Ibid.

Christian belief that we are situated, historical creatures and as such we are subject to the influences of the world around us, benign and malign. The early church was acutely aware of this, envisaging themselves, like Israel, as a community set apart by their righteous conduct and filial care for each other in order to witness to the new life that they had received in Christ. St. Paul's letters are filled with admonitions to right conduct and the cultivation of good habits, most notably in his exhortation to the Philippians: 'Finally, brethren, whatever things are true, whatever things are noble, whatever things are just, whatever things are pure, whatever things are lovely, whatever things are of good report, if there is any virtue and if there is anything praiseworthy, meditate on these things. The things you have learned and received and heard and saw in me, these do and the God of peace will be with you'. (Philippians 4:8 NKJV).

Like the early church, Burke recognised that an acknowledgement of Christianity's truths exercised a profound influence upon the manners and customs of a society. By 1790 Burke had noticed what he perceived to be a concomitant decline in morality alongside the decline of the Christian religion in France. In the name of reason the French revolutionaries had completely altered the institution of marriage, denying its divine origin and making it a civil contract. Burke wrote: 'The Christian religion, by confining marriage to pairs, and rendering the relation indissoluble, has by these two things done more toward the peace, happiness, settlement, and civilization of the world, than by any other part in this whole scheme of divine wisdom.'[58] In an age in which traditional social mores are scrutinised by an establishment which aims to reform in accordance to equality and human rights, Burke's defence of Christian institutions, which emerge from theological beliefs, seems particularly pertinent and reminds us that a society which is governed by a Christian culture looks distinctly different to that which emerges from the anthropological premises of the contractarian tradition.

This relationship between the institutional church and the state has been also been elaborated by a figure greatly influenced by Burke, namely Samuel Taylor Coleridge in his *On the Constitution of Church and State*.[59] For Coleridge, the role of the church included the diffusion

---

[58] Burke, 'Letters on a Regicide Peace', *The Works,* op. cit., Vol. XIII, p. 174.
[59] Samuel T. Coleridge, *On the Constitution of the Church and State* (1826) (Charleston, SC: Nabu Press, 2012).

of civil manners in all parts of society. Although Coleridge and Burke were both clear that a functional separation between the church and state was necessary, they nevertheless believed that the church had a central role to play in society. Such a belief was hardly novel. The Country Party championed by Bolingbroke in the 1740s, and supported by Swift and Samuel Johnson, inspired a conception of the church as an important third estate which should maintain an independent revenue so as to maintain its freedom. This was a belief which both Burke and Coleridge advocated strongly. Burke helped to inspire a strong Anglican tradition which echoed these beliefs, especially following the Reform Act of 1832. At the same time that Coleridge wrote his profoundly Burkean work on the church and state, Thomas Arnold authored *Principles of Church Reform*, and later political figures such as Disraeli and Gladstone championed the moral influence of the Church of England upon the nation. In the twentieth century this understanding of the church as the cultural centre of gravity for society was echoed by T.S. Eliot who saw 'culture [as] being, essentially, the incarnation (so to speak) of the religion of a people'.[60] All of these individuals emphasised the importance of the church institution in the belief that man was not an autonomous agent governed only by legislation, but rather a social creature shaped by customs, manners and institutions. For Burke, the healthy customs and manners of Britain emerged from the natural law and were supplemented by the civilising message of the Christian gospel as explained by the church.

Principle 6. *An emphasis on the role of civil society, subordinate affections and the nation state*

The great conservative statesman George Canning wrote: 'It is idle, it is mere pedantry… to overlook the affections of nature'.[61] This principle of conservatism is related to, yet distinct from, the conservative emphasis on customs. It springs from an acknowledgement of our creatureliness and the conviction that the natural bonds of civil society are integral to

[60] T.S. Eliot, *Notes towards the Definition of Culture* (London: Faber and Faber, 2nd Ed., 1962), p. 28.
[61] George Canning in 'The Anti-Jacobin Review and True Churchman's Magazine', Vol. XLVI (January to June 1814), p. 614.

human flourishing. Nigel Biggar offers a helpful theological account of the natural affections towards community, and in particular the nation as a locus of community:

> Christians should base their view of the nation on their understanding of human being as creaturely. This involves distinguishing it sharply from the universal and eternal being of God and taking seriously its historicality – that is, its boundedness by time and space. Humans come into being and grow up in a particular time, and if not in one particular place and community then in a limited number of them. Human individuals are normally nurtured, inducted into social life, and encouraged in certain self-understandings by their family and by other institutions – educational, religious, recreational, economic, and political – that mediate the history and ethos of their local and national communities. It is natural, therefore, that individuals should feel special affection for, and loyalty toward, those communities that have cared for them and given them so much that is beneficial; and, since beneficiaries ought to be grateful to benefactors, it is right that they should.[62]

Such an account would certainly have been agreeable to Burke who continually sought to reassert the humanity and creatureliness of human beings against the rationalism of the *philosophes*. It certainly resonates with Burke's own statements concerning our natural prejudices and seems to be implicit in his admonitions to accept our nature as social creatures in a community with others.

Burke perceived that in taking a conception of humanity as rational, equal and free to be axiomatic, the philosophy of the revolutionaries resulted in an inhumane and cold polity. Commenting on the relation between parents and their children Burke wrote: 'Your masters reject the duties of this vulgar relation, as contrary to liberty; as not founded in the social compact; and not binding according to the rights of men; because the relation is not, of course, the result of *free election*; never so on the

---

[62] Nigel Biggar, 'The Value of Limited Loyalty: Christianity, the Nation and Territorial Boundaries' in John A. Coleman, ed., *Christian Political Ethics* (Princeton, NJ: Princeton University Press, 2007), p. 93.

side of the children, not always on the part of the parents'.[63] Given his ostensible emphasis on feelings, it is perhaps unsurprising that Rousseau in particular, whom Burke called, 'a lover of his kind but a hater of his kindred',[64] came into Burke's firing line for a complete lack of feeling: 'It is that new invented virtue which your masters canonize, that led their moral hero constantly to exhaust the stores of his powerful rhetoric in the expression of universal benevolence; whilst his heart was incapable of harbouring one spark of common parental affection. Benevolence to the whole species, and want of feeling for every individual with whom the professors come in contact'.[65]

Burke was equally clear in identifying the roots of this unfeeling in the same vain esteem for human reason: 'The bear loves, licks, and forms her young; but bears are not philosophers. Vanity, however, finds its account in reversing the train of natural feelings. Thousands admire the sentimental writer; the affectionate father is hardly known in his parish'.[66]

In Joshua Hordern's *Political Affections*, he aims to approach 'the question of affections' in political relations from an explicitly theological direction'[67] and thus helps us to dissect the theological importance of parochial affections. In chapter three of the book Hordern explicitly cites Burke's statement that the rampant individualism of the revolutionaries is no basis for the construction of society:

Nothing is left which engages the affections on the part of the commonwealth. On the principles of this mechanic philosophy, our institutions can never be embodied, if I may use the expression, in persons, so as to create in us love, veneration, admiration, or attachment. But that sort of reason which banishes the affections is incapable of filling their place. These public affections, combined with manners, are required sometimes as supplements, sometimes as correctives, always as aids to law.[68]

---

[63] Burke, 'Letter to a member of the National Assembly', *The Works,* op. cit., Vol. VI, p. 35.

[64] Ibid.

[65] Ibid., p. 33.

[66] Ibid., p. 34.

[67] Joshua Hordern, *Political Affections: Civic Participation and Moral Theology* (Oxford University Press, 2013), p. 132.

[68] Burke, quoted in Hordern, *Political Affections,* op. cit., p. 132.

Hordern comments that Burke is 'imprecise' about the way in which such public affections are 'somehow vital to the personal, representative embodiment of institutions and the workings of law'.[69] Hordern is correct insofar as Burke does not offer an explicit account of the theological significance of the affections. For Burke, natural prejudices were part of what it was to be a created being and, as we have seen, he asserts their importance in the face of cold enlightenment rationalism. Burke did not, however, believe that prejudices and affections should be followed blindly. He believed them to be the glue which binds man to his fellow man but ultimately to, and subject to the laws, of God.

Burke had been aware of the necessity of the natural affections from an early age. He had reviewed Adam Smith's *Theory of Moral Sentiments* whilst working for Dodsley's *Annual Register* and, whilst expressing doubts as to the completeness of Smith's theory, Burke nevertheless believed it to be 'one of the most beautiful fabrics of moral theory, that has perhaps ever appeared'.[70] Similarly, in his *Vindication* he satirises the view that reason alone is sufficient for social order. For Burke, the affections should only be followed to the extent that they lead us to act in a manner which is in keeping with God's created order and subordinate to the divine law. As Stanlis puts it: the 'invisible tissue of loyalties and prejudices... gave cohesion and concreteness to the divine contract, which connected man in the eternal frame of the universe'.[71]

Burke provides an account of the way in which our affections are linked to effective participation and ultimately representative embodiment in institutions. We have seen that the natural law is what links subordinate affections to the nation at large, drawing us into expanding circles of communication and affection. For Burke, the benign effect of the natural law is the right ordering of society, and a well ordered society naturally leads humans from proximate affections to distant affections: 'To be attached to the subdivision, to love the little platoon we belong to in society, is the first principle (the germ as it were) of public affections. It is the first link in the series by which we proceed towards a love to

---

[69] Hordern, op cit., p. 132.
[70] Burke, quoted in David Bromwich, *The Intellectual Life of Edmund Burke* (London: Harvard University Press, 2014), p. 40.
[71] Stanlis, *Edmund Burke and the Natural Law*, op. cit., p. 84.

our country, and to mankind'.[72]

Hordern describes these affections as 'the participative beginnings of understanding',[73] involving an acknowledgement that we are contingent beings with situated backgrounds; in short we are from somewhere. The admission of this basic fact is helpful not least because it 'is directly opposed to an autarchic or self-sufficient view of life'.[74] Drawing on Lacoste, Hordern speaks of 'intentional, affective recognitions of value'.[75] In this account affections are not blind sentimentality, but the 'half-light of ethics' which identify values as 'the first ethical facts'.[76] In such a conception affections are 'the beginning of a process by which moral norms are disclosed'. As the 'half light' of ethics and the beginning of ethical understanding, Hordern suggests that within political communities the affections should be subject to a process of 'intersubjective verification'.[77] Moreover, 'through them we are drawn into a close attentiveness to what the world is like and to what we should do about it'; they are a 'deeply human way of... being attentive to reality'.[78] Hordern describes the affections as a 'creaturely, participatory form of knowing', arguing that these first affective 'recognitions of value' are the beginnings of us 'being knit into all that there is, when "all that there is" is interpreted as 'the moral order vindicated in Christ'.[79] This account holds much common ground with Burke's view of affections as the first link in the series of a divinely ordained order by which we are knit together with man and God.

In Burke's criticism of the revolutionary establishment he too draws this link between instinctive affections and virtue: 'The whole drift of their institution is contrary to that of the wise Legislators of all countries, who aimed at improving instincts into morals, and at grafting the virtues on the stock of the natural affections.'[80] It is significant that Burke laments that 'they dispose of all the family relations of parents and

---

[72] Burke, *Reflections on the Revolution in France*, op. cit., p. 100.
[73] Hordern, op cit., p. 62.
[74] Ibid.
[75] Ibid.
[76] Ibid.
[77] Ibid.
[78] Ibid.
[79] Ibid.
[80] Burke, 'Letters on a Regicide Peace', *The Works*, op. cit., Vol. XIII, p. 173.

children, husbands and wives' arguing that in so doing 'they corrupt the morals' of the people.[81] The following passage is particularly helpful in understanding the way in which Burke sees affections as ultimately leading us to God. It should be noted that the church (and its message) is not incidental in this process:

> First, I beg leave to speak of our church establishment, which is the first of our prejudices, not a prejudice destitute of reason, but involving in it profound and extensive wisdom. I speak of it first. It is first and last and midst in our minds. For, taking ground on that religious system of which we are now in possession, we continue to act on the early received and uniformly continued sense of mankind. That sense not only, like a wise architect, hath built up the august fabric of states, but, like a provident proprietor, to preserve the structure from profanation and ruin, as a sacred temple purged from all the impurities of fraud and violence and injustice and tyranny, hath solemnly and forever consecrated the commonwealth and all that officiate in it. This consecration is made that all who administer the government of men, in which they stand in the person of God himself, should have high and worthy notions of their function and destination, that their hope should be full of immortality, that they should not look to the paltry pelf of the moment nor to the temporary and transient praise of the vulgar, but to a solid, permanent existence in the permanent part of their nature, and to a permanent fame and glory in the example they leave as a rich inheritance to the world.
>
> Such sublime principles ought to be infused into persons of exalted situations, and religious establishments provided that may continually revive and enforce them. Every sort of moral, every sort of civil, every sort of politic institution, aiding the rational and natural ties that connect the human understanding and affections to the divine, are not more than necessary in order to build up that wonderful structure Man, whose prerogative it is to be in a great degree a creature of his own making, and who, when made as he ought to be made, is destined to hold no trivial place in the creation. But whenever man is put over men, as the better nature ought ever

[81] Burke 'Letter to a Member of the National Assembly', *The Works, op. cit.*, Vol. VI, p. 38.

to preside, in that case more particularly, he should as nearly as possible be approximated to his perfection.[82]

This passage could attract a wealth of commentary, but we might highlight three main points. First, the church is seen as 'the first of our prejudices' and Burke is careful to note that the esteem attributed to the church is 'not destitute of reason'. In this account the church plays an integral role in the right ordering of society, building up the fabric of states and consecrating society. The natural law exercised through prudential judgements may be central to Burke, but so is the church's message. Secondly, Burke is clear that society should be consecrated by the church's benign influence in order that those who administer human government (which is 'in the person of God himself') should be full of the hope of immortality. Burke's account of the function of hope is interwoven with the affections, directing man towards God in order that man should become what he ought to be. If they are invigorated by the hope afforded by such an eternal perspective, then they will 'leave a rich inheritance to the world'. Finally, Burke is clear that, in a rightly ordered society, moral, civil and political institutions work harmoniously to connect the natural human affections and understanding to the divine. It is notable that affections and understanding are coupled. For Burke, affections are not blind and senseless, but directed towards natural ends and thus, when rightly ordered, harmonious with reason and understanding.

For Burke then, there is a clear link and a mutually enriching harmony between the natural affections of created beings, the gospel message as disseminated by the church and the common grace of the natural law which informs our practical reason and our moral intuitions.

Summary

In this chapter we have identified six intersecting political principles in Burke's thought which emerge from his Christian faith. These political principles offer Christians one way of engaging with politics which avoids the dangers of ideology and preserves a space for God to act in the midst of difficult political questions. I have not argued that

---

[82] Ibid.

conservatism is the only body of political principles which might viably guide a Christian's approach to politics. However, I have defended the view that the core doctrinal commitments of the Christian faith are deeply woven into the Burkean conservative's worldview. Thus I believe Burkean conservatism to be an approach to politics which has much to offer a society which seems increasingly riven by a lack of corporate identity and moral clarity. Burke's natural law based constitutionalism offers an approach to politics which operates within a robust Christian framework while still advocating tolerance and epistemological humility. Such an approach allows us to remain humble and cautious as we discern a path through perilous political issues, yet it offers us clear reference points from which we must take our bearings. Without such a Christian framework on which to ground our ethical beliefs and adjudicate upon our cultural values, we can see that the rights-based reason of secular liberalism is not sufficient to engender a common concord amongst competing traditions.

Chapter Seven

Conservatism in the Modern World

We now turn to look in more detail at areas of public policy and ask how a Burkean approach to politics might affect the way we think about our public life today.

The relevance of the historical debates we have been looking at may seem distant from today's society, yet they are far more proximate than we might imagine. Our contemporary society, increasingly secular in nature, is rapidly re-orientating its moral bearings from the historically Christian understanding of a created moral order to a moral consensus focused upon human rights. The culture of justice, peace and respect to which I believe most liberal contractarian thinkers are aspiring is in reality jeopardised by the nature of their own political project. The foundational idea that humans are free agents, able to determine their own identity has clearly proved unsatisfactory for many in the West. Beyond Brexit in the UK and the election of Donald Trump in the US, we can see a desire across Europe for the reaffirmation of communal and cultural identities, particularly among working class communities. The rise of the Freedom party of Austria, the Front Nationale in France, the Alternative für Deutschland in Germany, as well as similar parties in Latvia, Hungary and Lithuania demonstrate that the social effects of cosmopolitanism, globalisation and multiculturalism are being rejected by significant portions of the population. Our human nature was created with a strong sense of locality and sociality. In this chapter I will look at how our public policy should acknowledge this fact and channel it positively, rather than continuing in the belief that human flourishing is best achieved by autonomy and self-determination. If a nation is to cohere, then it must have a sense of common identity and integral to this is a shared moral vision.

A shared moral vision

We have looked at the liberal hope of reconstituting a society by making equality and autonomy our ultimate cultural aspiration; this is realised both through the law and, perhaps more powerfully, through influencing the public discourse of the nation. The results of this have been far reaching and complex, but one effect has been the silencing of Britain's Christian culture.

In a court judgment of Lord Justice Laws in 2010, we can see the core premises which define the stream of liberalism which we have been looking at. One of the characteristic features of liberalism is that unverifiable faith claims are regarded as subjective and therefore hold no place in the public sphere. Lord Justice Laws was clear that faith claims have no place in the central institutions of government and should not receive any public privilege. For him, it is only to the extent that a particular claim is coherent as a 'social or moral position' and commends itself by reason that it can have any traction in law. All law must ultimately rest upon objective grounds of right reason and not 'subjective' religious beliefs. It is both 'irrational' as well as 'divisive, capricious and arbitrary' to derive laws from purely religious beliefs. Therefore 'the precepts of any one religion' cannot 'sound any louder in the general law than the precepts of any other'. The state must rationally 'think for itself' as a 'free and rational regime'. For this tradition of liberalism, reason and the rights of the individual are paramount. Such rights, enshrined in British law since 1998, must trump considerations of precedent, national character and articles of religious faith.

Lord Justice Laws' view that religion ought to be a private matter which is entirely separate from the rationality of the state does not account for the fact that the Christian religion has for centuries occupied a privileged constitutional position in Great Britain. Furthermore, Britain's institutions and laws in fact emerge from a particular religious tradition which is not self-evidently or 'objectively' reasonable outside of that tradition.[1] We are entitled to ask: upon what first premises does the ostensibly detached reason of the state operate? Are all religious claims which cannot be empirically verified to be regarded as subjective,

---

[1] See Nigel Biggar, 'Why the 'establishment' of the Church of England is Good for a Liberal Society', in Mark Chapman, Judith Maltby, William Whyte (eds.), *The Established Church: Past, Present and Future* (London: T & T Clark, 2011).

irrational or private beliefs? These are important questions which will increasingly demand a response as the secular establishment moves further away from the Christian heritage of the nation's past.

As we have seen, Lord Justice Laws' judgment is at odds with the understanding of the constitutional order articulated by significant figures in the British political and legal traditions. His account of the British constitution would have been unrecognisable to the leading lawyers of the past. Following Lord Justice Laws' judgment, the former Archbishop of Canterbury George Carey reflected:

> As I read those words I realized how different my world view is from that of this learned judge and, at the same time, how ill-informed he was about the Christian tradition – and even less informed about the way that Christian faith is woven into the history, culture, ethics, laws and political life of the United Kingdom.[2]

Carey proceeds to think back to the Queen's coronation in 1953: 'where the Queen was presented with a Bible: "To keep your Majesty ever mindful of the Law and the Gospel as the rule for the whole of life and government of Christian princes."' Carey reflects that 'Those powerful and precise words were not designed as a commitment binding on the young queen alone; they were intended to signal that what our country stood for was a commitment to Christian values and teaching that stemmed from our foundational document.'[3]

There has never been a time in British history in which a wholly unified moral vision has governed the nation, but what is crucial to a country's progress is that there are commonly held sources of authority by which to advance contemporary debates. The loss of the moral vision that had emerged from the Christian tradition has resulted in a variety of symptoms in our society. Perhaps the most notable has been the rise of political correctness.

---

[2] George Carey and Andrew Carey, *We Don't do God: The Marginalisation of Public Faith* (Oxford: Monarch Books, 2012), pp. 13-14.
[3] Ibid., pp. 14-15.

Political Correctness

The secularisation of the public sphere has manifested itself in a variety of ways. From Locke to Rawls, we have seen that equality is a watchword of the liberal tradition. Just as the French revolutionaries changed their calendar and holidays to reflect the dawn of reason, so modern liberals seem intent on stripping Britain of those aspects of its public life that are distinctly Christian, advancing their agenda under an ostensible desire for equality. Whether on radio, in schools or on television, Christianity's cultural primacy has rapidly diminished. Examples of this abound. Recently, the US city of Bloomington Indiana renamed Good Friday as Spring Holiday in the belief that to have a Christian holiday would not be sufficiently inclusive. In Oxford England in 2008 the City Council decided to rename the Christmas light parade a 'Winter light festival'.

As well-meaning, or not, as such gestures may be, the liberal attempt to carve out a neutral public sphere will inevitably fail, for the very reasons that Burke identified over two hundred years ago. The state cannot simply pretend that it does not hold its own moral vision over and above those of other religious traditions. When it becomes clear that it does, it too must justify the cultural primacy of that position in the market place of beliefs. Similarly, the religious commitment of individuals will inevitably hold implications for their lives in the public square. As our society departs ever further from its Christian roots, the state's moral vision may become sufficiently removed from the traditional values of some communities that a serious conflict of loyalties may arise. Indeed, on particular issues and for certain individuals and organisations, this is already the case in America and Britain. The realisation that accepting the primacy of liberalism's account of man and society will inevitably be to the detriment of the Christian religion in Britain was something which Burke perceived long before his time.

The state-owned BBC offers a good example of an ostensibly impartial government organisation. In the first half of the twentieth century, when Britain's Christian culture still predominated, the BBC transparently reflected these values. Indeed in the BBC entrance hall there is an inscription, placed there in 1932, which reads 'This temple of the arts and muses is dedicated to Almighty God'. In the intervening years there has been a marked shift to a deeply liberal organisation.

The BBC has been accused of anti-Christian bias, perhaps because it sees Christianity as a soft target that won't bite back. In a 2011 survey, BBC viewers complained that Christians are routinely depicted in a derogatory fashion, while 'minority religions are better represented despite Christianity being the most widely observed religion in Britain'.[4] Peter Sissons, a BBC anchor for twenty years, relates how at the BBC 'Islam must not be offended at any price, although Christians are fair game because they do nothing about it if they are offended.' He claims that there is an entrenched mind set of liberal bias within the organisation and the political spin is dictated by *The Guardian* and *The Independent*, stating that 'producers refer to them routinely'. He goes on to say that he 'lost count of the number of times I asked a producer for a brief on a story, only to be handed a copy of *The Guardian*'. Sissons notes that there is a political line on everything of importance, that 'percolates subtly throughout the organisation'. For instance, 'Whatever the United Nations is associated with is good – it is heresy to question any of its activities. The EU is also a good thing'. In politics 'Obama was not just the Democratic Party's candidate for the White House, he was the BBC's.'[5] Sissons' memoirs paint a bleak portrait of an organisation purporting to be impartial. They remind us that the liberal state can never be impartial, because liberalism possesses its own system of beliefs.

The liberalism of the eighteenth century should make Christians far more wary about ceding the public square to the competing moral vision of the liberal tradition. Elements of the Church of England have been guilty of mistaking the liberal message of natural rights, equality and autonomy, for the gospel. In 2015 the Rev Giles Goddard, 'a prominent liberal cleric', held an Islamic Prayer Service in a Christian Church in Waterloo. It is not hard to detect the influence of liberalism in such misguided ventures. The liberal tendency to emphasise the absolute equality of all religions makes it impossible to make claims as to the primacy of truthfulness in any one religion. This is a short step from

---

[4] BBC Survey quoted in 'BBC is anti-Christian and ageist, viewer survey finds', http://www.telegraph.co.uk/news/religion/8549315/BBC-is-anti-Christian-and-ageist-viewer-survey-finds.html (accessed 12th February, 2017).
[5] Peter Sissons, quoted in 'Left Wing Bias? It's written through the BBC's very DNA, says Peter Sissons', http://www.dailymail.co.uk/news/article-1349506/Left-wing-bias-Its-written-BBCs-DNA-says-Peter-Sissons.html (accessed 15th February, 2017).

the sort of syncretistic prayer service which treats religions as not only equal in status, but equal in content to the point of homogeneity. The Christian belief that Jesus Christ is a person of the triune Godhead is incompatible with the claim that he is a prophet of Allah. While it is logically impossible that Allah is the same God as that worshipped by Christians, Reverend Giles purportedly stated 'we all share these great traditions, so let us celebrate our shared traditions, by giving thanks to the God that we love, Allah'. Benevolence and respect for other faiths is not the same as agreement with their beliefs. Wilfully expediting the establishment of liberal ideas may prove to be a grave mistake for the Church of England. Authenticity and integrity will ultimately distinguish the Church far more than a slavish acquiescence to contemporary trends.

Multiculturalism

Under the Blair administration the idea of multiculturalism was given a clear voice. As late as 2006, Blair spoke of Britain being 'at ease' with different cultures, celebrating the fact that 'the stuffy Old Britain' had passed away. He continued to say that 'no distinctive culture or religion supersedes our duty to be part of an integrated United Kingdom'. The basis of Blair's argument was that, so long as we all agree that we ought to be tolerant because humans are bearers of rights, then all cultures can thrive in Britain contemporaneously. In the same speech he articulated the view that beyond thin values such as 'tolerance' and 'equal treatment for all', the primacy of British culture did not really matter.[6] The failing in this view is that toleration and respect are products of a nation's culture and that this is moulded by religious belief. This was Burke's central contention when arguing against the liberals' attempt to create a society upon their vision of man. Their vision of man as free, equal and a bearer of rights, was a product of a particular history and a particular culture and yet they were using it to dispense with the very culture from which it had emerged.

Andrew Neather, a one-time adviser to Tony Blair, relates how the policy of multiculturalism was an intentional attempt 'to rub the right's nose in diversity and render their arguments out of date'. Yet the plan

---

[6] Tony Blair, 'Our Nation's Future: Multiculturalism and integration', speech delivered on 8th December, 2006.

backfired and Blair's policy of mass immigration ultimately resulted in the failure of whole communities to integrate into British society. In 2016 Dame Louise Casey was commissioned by the government to conduct a review into opportunity and integration in the UK. Her review found that communities in areas such as Bradford, Birmingham and Blackburn, were comprised of up to 85% Muslims of Pakistani or Bangladeshi origin. Troublingly, in communities which had over 20% Muslim residents, some of the values exhibited were markedly and worryingly different from those of the rest of the population. The report states that, 'Too many public institutions, national and local, state and non-state, have gone so far to accommodate diversity and freedom of expression that they have ignored or even condoned regressive, divisive and harmful cultural and religious practices, for fear of being branded racist or Islamophobic.' [7]

In 2011 David Cameron made a speech in Munich in which he gave a frank assessment of the failure of 'the doctrine of state multiculturalism', arguing that 'we have even tolerated these segregated communities behaving in ways that run counter to our values'. The former Chief Rabbi, Jonathan Sacks, wrote an article in 2011 agreeing with David Cameron's assessment that multiculturalism is a failed enterprise. Sacks relates how his parents 'admired the British for their tolerance and decency', noting that 'They were proud to be English because the English were proud to be English.' As Sacks points out, 'in the absence of pride there can be no identity at all'. In a multicultural society the fetishisation of difference is unsurprisingly corrosive of the commonalities that constitute a nation. He makes the point that his parents 'integrated and encouraged us to go further because there was something to integrate into'. [8]

The attempt to forge a multicultural society failed because a society needs to feel itself to be a society. The perception of a shared heritage, history and trajectory, create the sinews of kinship that facilitate the muscle movements of democracy. Citizens must know and care about

---

[7] Louise Casey, 'The Casey Review: A review into opportunity and integration', https://www.gov.uk/government/uploads/system/uploads/attachment_data/file/575973/The_Casey_Review_Report.pdf (accessed 20th January, 2017), p. 70.
[8] Jonathan Sacks, 'Giving and belonging: The lesson Jews can offer new immigrants', http://rabbisacks.org/giving-and-belonging-the-lesson-jews-can-offer-new-immigrants/ (accessed 21st January, 2017).

their fellow citizens and feel that in some sense their fates are interlinked, an idea captured in the phrase *E Pluribus Unum* (out of many, one). Most important to this is that a society must have a shared moral vision. It is a shared moral vision above all else that will determine the trajectory of a nation. The contemporaneous growth of separate cultures holding widely divergent systems of values simply cannot co-exist under the same body of law and in the same public institutions. Our laws, institutions and economies are a product of our values. This is why the promotion of values must have primacy of place if a nation is to succeed. As Jonathan Sacks writes, 'You cannot have a society without a shared moral code.'

It must be emphasised that a rejection of multiculturalism must never be confused with a rejection of multi-ethnicism. Britain has always been, and will always be a home to men and women of all ethnicities. Just as Polish Jews during World War Two became some of the most patriotic British citizens, so today immigrants continue to come to Britain with a love for her history and culture, and indeed they provide a valuable contribution to her ever evolving culture. (This is quite different from encouraging different cultures to develop within one nation contemporaneously.) Racism remains the ugly face of the far right, defining identity according to the mirage of racial homogeneity. Burke's insight was that a nation coheres because of the social ties and beliefs that connect individuals to a community, not because of an ethnic identity. It should also be clear that the desire for a broadly Christian culture does not preclude the peaceful and fruitful coexistence of other religions. As Jonathan Sacks notes, 'tolerance ignores differences; multiculturalism makes an issue of them at every point'.[9] It is the Christian culture of Britain that should provide the basis for toleration.

Toleration

Compassion and care for those of minority faith groups has been a part of the conservative tradition since the time of Burke. Yet it should be stressed that Christians ought not to care for those of other faiths because they doubt the veracity of their own. It is not on the basis of epistemic uncertainty that the other is loved, but rather it is the article of faith which constitutes the bedrock of the Christian love for the other.

[9] Sacks, op. cit.

The inescapable corollary of this is that, from a Christian perspective, the public square will flourish most fully if it is founded on a distinctly Christian moral vision.

If Christian politicians, public figures and above all the church believe what they profess, then they ought to be unequivocal that the British common law has more justice in it than the Sharia, the Gospels a greater degree of revelation than the Torah, Christianity's account of man more virtue than that of Hinduism. This does not mean that no virtue can be seen in other religious positions, but Christians ought to regard their religion as the wellspring of cultural toleration, not just a beneficiary.

Burke was clear on this point. He wrote that, 'The teachers who reformed our religion in England' were 'sincere believers; men of the most fervent and exalted piety'. Such men realised 'that justice and mercy are substantial parts of religion', and therefore they did not practice cruelty towards those who did not share their faith. Burke contrasted this Christian toleration, founded upon a faith which commends justice and mercy, with the toleration of the liberals, whose supercilious attitude towards faith allowed religions to exist within the confines that liberalism defined. Burke was clear as to what he made of the liberal profession of tolerance towards all religions:

> We hear these new teachers continually boasting of their spirit of toleration. That those persons should tolerate all opinions, who think none to be of estimation, is a matter of small merit. Equal neglect is not impartial kindness.[10]

Having an established Christian religion gives faith a special place in society, particularly given that the monarch remains the Church's political figurehead. Moreover, the established church emphasises a toleration rooted in the belief that all humans have an innate dignity as God's creation.

By contrast, there are elements of the liberal tradition today that show remarkably little tolerance to those with whom they disagree. We have seen how in the eighteenth century the liberal tradition's belief in human reason led to a intolerance towards those it deemed unreasonable. On university campuses and in the media we can observe a burgeoning

[10] Burke, *Reflections on the Revolution in France*, op. cit., p. 273.

intolerance towards dissent from liberal viewpoints.

At Christ Church college, Oxford, two speakers were invited to debate abortion by Oxford Students for Life. However, because both speakers were male, there was an outcry among campus feminists who said such a debate threatened the mental welfare of students. Christ Church called off the event. At the University of Exeter in 2006, the Christian Union was excluded from the student guild and had its bank account frozen after it asked members to sign a statement of religious belief. Similarly, at the University of Birmingham, it was deemed that requiring the leaders of the Christian Union to be Christian was not sufficiently inclusive. The Student Union also criticised the Christian Union's constitution for using the terms 'men' and 'women', which it did not believe were sufficiently gender inclusive. Politicians and public figures with whom students disagree politically have been banned from speaking at major universities,[11] while in university lectures and debates, individuals are being asked to issue warnings before discussing topics that might trigger negative feelings for other students.[12] Such a cotton wool culture stems from a worldview in which the individual's rights are paramount. Excessive individualism risks leading to the suppression of truth, because truth is seen as subordinate to the feelings of individuals.

The lack of tolerance increasingly exhibited by student liberals was well illustrated at Middlebury College, Vermont in 2017. The controversial political theorist Charles Murray was drowned out by student activists as he attempted to give an address. As a result he was forced to speak via a live stream in a private room. In response, students triggered the buildings fire alarms. As Professor Murray and a Middlebury faculty member, Professor Allison Stranger, attempted to leave the college, they were confronted by a violent group of students who manhandled them. Stranger was assaulted, her hair was pulled and her neck twisted, to the extent that she needed medical attention at a hospital. Murray and Stranger were escorted to a vehicle, which was subsequently set upon by violent protestors, rocking it and pounding it.

---

[11] In recent years, attempts have been made by students and NUS officials to prevent a wide variety of public figures speaking, including: Germaine Greer, Boris Johnson, Tony Benn, George Galloway and Julian Assange.

[12] Matthew Scott, http://www.telegraph.co.uk/news/2016/05/11/trigger-warnings-at-oxford-would-threaten-academic-freedom-and-i/, (accessed 21st February, 2017).

Prior to the lecture, a letter had circulated the campus, signed by over 500 alumni, stating that Murray's presence was 'a threat... to every woman, every person of colour, every first-generation student, every poor and working class person, every disabled person and every queer person'. Irrespective of what one thinks of an academic's work, it is a worrying state of affairs when such censorious behaviour becomes normalised.[13]

In a similar incident in 2016, the Canadian Professor, Jordan Peterson, refused to use gender neutral pronouns such as 'ze' and 'zir'. The University of Toronto warned that, in doing so, he may be in breach of the human rights of trans individuals. The incident also resulted in a protest at the University of Toronto, in which Professor Peterson was drowned out by white noise played through speakers by students. Professor Peterson wrote in a statement to the BBC that he had studied authoritarian movements 'for a very long time – for 40 years – and they're started by people's attempts to control the ideological and linguistic territory'. He went on to say 'there's no way I'm going to use words made up by people who are doing that – not a chance'. In his view, gender arguments are being used by 'radical social constructionists', and the threat of human rights offences is being used to intimidate those they disagree with.[14]

Is it any surprise that a system of belief which elevates the self above all other things has produced a deeply egocentric society? Any belief which challenges the notion that the individual ought to be entirely autonomous and able to choose their own identity is vehemently decried. As Burke perceived, a society which sees rights as sacrosanct risks neglecting all of the other aspects of a healthy, functioning society. Individuals are told they have a right not to be offended, a right to live how they want and a right to choose their identity. Faced with high levels of substance abuse, the highest teenage pregnancy rates in Western Europe, rising depression levels, rising levels of loneliness and record obesity levels, it is hard to avoid the conclusion that the utter liberation of the human will has led to elements of our culture becoming deeply

[13] In Yale, 2015, Professor Nicholas Christakis and his wife were harassed by students for publishing a letter saying that they wonder whether the university was being too heavy handed in its prescription of acceptable Halloween costumes. Some students complained that freedom was less important than their feelings.

[14] Jessica Murphy, 'Toronto professor Jordan Petersen takes on gender neutral pronouns', http://www.bbc.co.uk/news/world-us-canada-37875695, (accessed 15th January 2017).

unhealthy. It would seem that the liberal tradition's assessment that human will is basically good is open to serious question.

Extremism

Where many believers of all faiths may in practice be able to comply with the liberal emphasis on religious neutrality in the public sphere, it is doubtful that more militant ideologies will be so acquiescent. Indeed, a public sphere increasingly devoid of articulations of faith may give a greater resonance to those strident voices who use violence to defy the liberal society's requirement for a neutral public sphere. The most prominent of these religious beliefs is a radical Islamic ideology that has filled the newspaper headlines with beheadings, crucifixions, the imposition of sharia and the subjugation of women. As Michael Nazir-Ali writes: 'Not since the demise of Marxism has the world been faced with a comprehensive political, social and economic ideology determined, by force if necessary, to achieve hegemony over large parts of the world. I mean, of course, the rise of radical Islamism'.[15]

In June 2014 the Prime Minister David Cameron wrote an article in the Sunday Times in response to the news that a group of Muslim schools in Birmingham had attempted to indoctrinate children with strict Islamic teachings. In the article Cameron insisted on the need to extol Britain's history, traditions and national character:

In recent years we have been in danger of sending out a worrying message: that if you don't want to believe in democracy, that's fine; that if equality isn't your bag, don't worry about it; that if you're completely intolerant of others, we will still tolerate you.

As I've said before, this has not just led to division, it has also allowed extremism – of both the violent and non-violent kind – to flourish…

So I believe we need to be far more muscular in promoting British values and the institutions that uphold them.

Cameron was explicit about the values he was referring to and went to lengths to stress their historical grounding in the British narrative:

[15] Michael Nazir-Ali, *Triple Jeopardy for the West* (London: Bloomsbury, 2012), p. 82.

We are bringing proper narrative history back to the curriculum, so our children really learn our island's story – and where our freedoms and things like our Parliament and constitutional monarchy came from.

Yet providing a historical narrative for such values does not authenticate them as good values. Without a common theological belief in a given order of justice, it is hard to offer a comprehensive account of why the British constitution is any more just than the Islamic Republic of Iran or the monarchy of Saudi Arabia. Indeed, a Wahhabist Muslim may well argue that Saudi Arabia's adherence to the Sharia makes it a far more just country than the United Kingdom. Herein lies the difficulty. Cameron's rhetoric seems to rest upon the same supposition which we saw in Locke, the *Philosophes* and Rawls. Namely that there is such thing as a universal and abstract mode of reason which is capable of operating outside of any substantial metaphysical commitments. The assumption is that if a human is reasonable then he can be led to see the reasonability of liberal values. Thus Cameron states:

The values I'm talking about – a belief in freedom, tolerance of others, accepting personal and social responsibility, respecting and upholding the rule of law – are the things we should try to live by every day.

One cannot help be reminded of Bishop Nazir-Ali's caution:

The scramblings and scratchings-around of politicians and of elements in the media for 'values' which would provide ammunition in this battle are… extremely thin gruel and hardly adequate for the task before us.[16]

As the life of 21st Century Britain rolls on, we may find that the beleaguered cry for a return to distinctively British values is not enough. Such values may be dismissed as merely incidental peculiarities of British history and, as such, may be washed away by more malign influences unless we reaffirm the Burkean belief that the peculiar values which our nation has enjoyed are distinctively Christian. With Nazir-Ali

[16] Nazir-Ali, op cit., p. 8.

one might raise the question as to whether such thin values have the spiritual resources to satisfy the core of the human condition, which the conservative tradition has long maintained is spiritual in nature.

A danger of the liberal project is not that it will prove too strong but that it will prove too weak. With the rise of militant Islam and far right groups in Britain, the autonomy of liberalism has created a vacuum of identity for many young men. In the years ahead we may see an increasing number of people drawn towards tight knit communities, with rich traditions and compelling historical narratives that can offer them meaning. Unless we can re-engage such people with a distinctive story, an identity and a moral vision, then we should not be surprised when they look for answers elsewhere.

Sadly, the liberal tradition is by nature unprepared to meet the challenge of radical groups offering disillusioned men and women a sense of meaning. In its absolute confidence in reason, it has failed to take seriously the religious beliefs of others. Following the Paris terror attacks, Theresa May told the British people these attacks 'were nothing to do with Islam'. Similarly, when the British soldier Lee Rigby was beheaded, his killer, Michael Adelbolajo stated 'I killed Lee Rigby because I am a soldier of Allah', yet the British people were told by David Cameron that the attack was nothing to do with the Islamic faith. Similar responses recur; when an Islamic terrorist attack is perpetrated a flurry of statements are issued by the media, politicians and public figures that such attacks have nothing to do with religion. The desire to prevent domestic tensions is admirable, but the reality is that these attacks have everything to do with a particular interpretation of Islam. What Western politicians are failing to understand is that a belief in human beings as free, equal, bearers of natural rights is not the theologically neutral position that many of our leaders assume it to be. It is a distinct metaphysical claim that radical Islamists simply do not agree with. Simply insisting, as Rawls does, that if you are reasonable you will agree with the claims of liberalism, is no different to a Christian telling an Islamist that if they were reasonable they would agree with the claims of Christ. The solution to such issues must be one which takes seriously the theological narratives that compel such acts and counters them with something more than the thin liberal account of man. If we fail to take seriously the religious beliefs which inspire such attacks then tackling such ideologies will be far harder in the long term.

Law and Rights

We have seen a variety of issues arising in relation to the idea of subjectively held rights. We have seen that at their worst they have been used to create a society that is radically individualistic. In the French Revolution, this individualism eventually gave rise to the tyranny of the general will. We have seen that the idea of secular natural rights was supposed to create a point of mutual consent between different factions, but ultimately they became a doctrine which bred an arrogant intolerance towards those with a different world view. We have seen the (false) liberal belief that rights emerged from reason alone, and should therefore sweep aside inherited traditions and beliefs.

This belief is as pervasive in the liberal tradition today as it was in revolutionary France. It is not hard to see how such a belief can very quickly restructure the cultural landscape of a nation. The assertion of sacrosanct, inalienable rights, though it purports to be founded upon reason, in fact makes a metaphysical claim, as opposed to a contextual legal claim, regarding the human person. The implication of this is as subtle, yet as important, as it was in the eighteenth century. Because such rights are seen as a constituent part of the human person, the right is seen as universal in scope so as not to degrade that individual's personhood. The right therefore comes to outweigh custom, tradition and precedent and overrides cultural and contextual considerations.

To give an example, does a murderer who has deprived others of their existence, have an inherent right to family life? If we are to believe the European Court of Human Rights (ECHR), then under article 8 of the European Convention on Human Rights they do. Similarly, British courts have traditionally refused prisoners the right to vote. The traditional argument is that we live in a society that is governed by laws and that, if an individual forsakes the law for their own ends, then they forsake the right to determine the law. In other words, the right to vote is not part of what it is to be human, it is a privilege contingent on British citizenship. The European Court of Human Rights has, however, repeatedly ordered the British parliament to extend some voting privileges to prisoners, arguing that their human rights are being violated. This case gives one example of the way in which the assertion of human rights has the capacity to restructure the legal and cultural landscape of a nation. By asserting an inherent right, liberal rights proponents do not need to make a case based on culture, common sense or ethical precedent; instead they have a trump card which allows them to brand any measure that opposes the advance of ostensible human rights as an opponent of humanity itself.

Human rights legislation in Britain has resulted in a series of profound changes in British public life; it has also resulted in a number of seeming contraventions of common sense. In particular, article 8 of the European Convention on Human Rights (the right to private and family life) has attracted a great deal of negative publicity for being used by foreign criminals seeking to avoid deportation at the expense of the British taxpayer. Such examples help to shed light on the issue of sacrosanct rights, in which the rights of the individual are divorced from all considerations of circumstance. The common law, originating in royal writs which evolved into courts of equity, has always been deeply concerned with the particularity of circumstances and has given the judge significant scope for interpretation. As a result the legal character of Britain has largely been shaped by circumstantial deliberation upon precedent as opposed to the abstract assertion of rights.

Increasingly today, those who oppose liberalism's march towards 'progress' are often branded as bigots or worse. In the wake of the vote to leave the European Union, there was a noted outpouring of vitriol on social media towards members of the elder generation (some of whom had fought for the country). The call for a second vote, or any way to overturn the referendum result, was sounded most prominently by the Liberal Democrat leader Tim Farron. It appeared to show a contempt for the opinions of the majority of voters. A belief in democracy was seemingly overshadowed by the liberal disdain for any who were not reasonable according to the ideas of liberal progressives.

There is a similar story to be told in the USA. As one commentator put it: 'There is a smug style in American liberalism. It has been growing these past decades. It is a way of conducting politics, predicated on the belief that American life is not divided by moral difference or policy divergence – not really – but by the failure of half the country to know what's good for them.' He proceeds to write that this attitude amounts to a 'defensive sneer towards any person or movement outside of its consensus, dressed up as a monopoly of reason.'[17] Those who have questioned the liberal agenda on a variety of ethical issues are consistently demonised in the media and on social media because they are perceived as opponents of reason, individual autonomy and natural rights. The vitriol of the liberal reaction to such opponents causes one to question whether it is an attempt to conceal the insecurity at the core of the tradition: that liberalism too rests on a series of distinctive metaphysical claims, which are neither rationally self-evident, nor empirically demonstrable.

Foreign policy

In the liberal tradition we saw a faith in human reason to construct a perfect system of government. We also saw the belief that all individuals are, at root, bearers of natural rights who desire to be free and equal. Such beliefs have animated the foreign policy of the west for decades. While there was a legitimate case to depose the tyrannical dictator Saddam Hussein, there was naiveté in assuming that the men and women of Iraq would subsequently desire liberal democracy as a substitute. After much blood and treasure has been expended, it has become apparent that seeing the citizens of Iraq simply as rights bearers, without any consideration of their culture, context or religion, was a terrible mistake.

For the Burkean there is, of course, an objective order of justice to which all rulers are accountable. But two considerations mitigate against triumphalist crusades to foreign lands. First, a Christian eschatology reminds us that the world is not marching towards a utopian order of reason, but rather it is enduring the 'beginning of birth pains' (Matthew 24:8).

Secondly, a Christian anthropology that reminds us that our own discernment is flawed and our vision is fragmentary. The result is a mode of foreign policy that is respectful of order where it is found, but when it does seek to intervene, it does so cautiously and prudentially,

---

[17] Emmit Rensin, 'The Smug Style in American Liberalism',
http://www.vox.com/2016/4/21/11451378/smug-american-liberalism
(accessed February 18th, 2017).

in the knowledge that all solutions are likely to be partial.

Community and the limits of the state

In an age of commuting, virtual communities and global citizenship, it is easy to see why people might crave a sense of authentic community and identity. The advance of the internet may have spawned virtual communities, but is it eroding the actual communities that we live in? The deep flaw with the idea of virtual communities is that in large part they are communities tailored by us, and for us. De-friending anyone who has dissimilar views to us, or who offends our sensibilities, can be done at the click of a button. In this sense virtual communities are communities in a very superficial sense. Such virtual communities don't force individuals to engage with those who are different from themselves. By contrast, real communities force us to confront the other, replete with all their foibles and offensive idiosyncrasies. They allow us to encounter a diverse array of characters and viewpoints, and moreover we are exposed to the judgements of others, and our sharp edges chastened by such socialisation. Through this process we learn to coexist with others, loving our neighbours in spite of divergent views, or peculiar habits. The parish church offers us a picture of a community in which rich and poor, educated and uneducated, kneel in the same pews and receive the same bread and wine. Yet, it is now possible to lead an existence sanitised of everyday interactions with other people. Encounters with the butcher, the baker and the librarian can all be circumvented by the internet. This raises the serious question as to whether it will much harder for individuals who increasingly construct their own worlds to become fully socialised individuals who have compassion for those different from themselves.

In a study conducted by psychological scientists from New York University, they examined a data set of over 150 million tweets. They discovered that on overtly political topics, Twitter became ideologically polarized. In other words, users would only read and repost material that reinforced their position.[18] One might speculate that this will ultimately prove deeply unhealthy for democracies, which rely on individuals ironing out their differences in the public square. At the very least,

---

[18] Pablo Barberá, John T. Jost, Jonathan Nagler, Joshua A. Tucker, and Richard Bonneau 'Tweeting From Left to Right: Is Online Political Communication More than an Echo Chamber', in Psychological Science Vol. 26, Issue 10 (August, 2015), pp. 1531 – 1542.

democracies require an empathy for our fellow citizens on the basis that we know and care for them. If we simply do not encounter those with different views from us in our everyday lives, it seems likely that this will ultimately give rise to intolerance. There is certainly a host of positive aspects to our digitally connected world, but if such networks aren't tempered by real communities, then they may give rise to a more narcissistic and less tolerant world.

It is not just the virtual world that has the potential to erode civic society. State welfare is a blessing for which we should be grateful. It provides the desperately poor with a safety net and it would be foolish entirely to dismiss its virtues. Yet, even seemingly good measures can have negative consequences and so must have their limitations. An over-extended system of welfare has the capacity to breed a dependence on the state and erode the everyday acts of community between citizens that help to foster a healthy society. In our modern society, it is easy to forget the correlation between the work of our neighbours and our own wellbeing. The liberal vision of humans as autonomous individuals who are not dependent on their fellow citizens is able to flourish when we forget that it is the hard work of our fellow citizens (whether or not we like or agree with them) that helps to pay for infrastructure, healthcare and the education of our children. During the recession the conservative party was forced to cut government expenditure and, as a result, food banks run by local churches filled the gaps left by the welfare state. While it is right to insist that governments do have a responsibility for the welfare of their citizens, the provision of help between fellow citizens is precisely the kind of civic transaction that strengthens the bonds of communities and should be encouraged by governments in conjunction with their own distribution of welfare.

Before the 2010 General Election the conservative party promoted the idea of the 'Big Society'. While such an idea is profoundly conservative, it is arguably not the government's place to tell people to engage with civic associations, and the project was largely perceived to fail. Yet the idea was an important one. A society that is more interdependent will ultimately be a closer and more robust society. This does not mean that government services need to be stripped back until we are dependent on our neighbours, but through community initiatives, sports, charities and associations we can, and should, strive to foster a more interconnected society.

Economic Policy

Capitalism in its extreme forms goes hand in hand with liberalism, insofar as it aims to maximise the absolute autonomy of the individual. This synthesis between liberal political theory and capitalism is known as neo-liberalism. We have seen that Locke believed freedom to be simply a lack of physical coercion. It was not the Christian freedom, with its implied duties, written about by Aquinas or Luther. In recent years we have seen the pitfalls in the view that individuals are autonomous agents who do not have any duties or obligations to their fellow citizens beyond those inscribed in law.

One of the chief grievances expressed by many working class Westerners is that those responsible for the financial crash went unpunished and continue to enjoy inflated salaries and bonuses. Contrary to the orthodoxy of the liberal tradition, the choices of individuals can have serious consequences for their fellow citizens. Burke's understanding of politics as a moral art, not a science, has much to say to modern economics. In its early years economics too was seen to be a moral art. One of Adam Smith's most famous works, which laid the foundations for his economic arguments, is his *Theory of Moral Sentiments*. Even during the late nineteenth century economics in Cambridge was found in a tripos alongside ethics. However, the professionalization of economics has led to a number of consequences. The neat curves and geometrical predictions of neo-classical economics assume the rationality of its agents and ultimately offers an account of man as a calculating machine. Of course, such assumptions failed to predict the economic crash precisely because they failed to account for the fact that man is not rational. While fields such as behavioural economics have gone some way to rectifying this failing, we must always be careful that our economic policy is cognizant of the messy world of human actions and motivations. In short we must be prudent as to the nature of capitalism: a force for good, if it is governed properly and channelled to serve moral ends.

Ultimately, there are a number of considerations that should govern our economic policy beyond the maximisation of Gross Domestic Product. While the vitality of commerce and industry is clearly necessary for a healthy society, it is rarely sufficient. For a culture to succeed it must value more than material wealth. It is this conviction that ought to unify those both on the left and the right who have become disillusioned with a liberal culture that seeks to realise the wellbeing of humankind through material acquisition.

Those promoting economic policies must always be mindful of their effects upon human character, society and communities. For example, it was considered the orthodoxy of the West that the combination of free trade and cheap credit is a good, because it increases choice and maximises the autonomy of individuals. But is there any evidence that the provision of endless commodities to consumers makes them happier? In fact the opposite seems to be true. In a study conducted by psychologist Barry Schwartz, he argues that in the modern world the sheer abundance of consumer choice we have is increasingly leading to depression and unhappiness.[19] Moreover, in the long term what are the effects of a nation glutting itself on cheap credit and running a trade deficit with its competitors? America's relationship with China since the 1990s serves as a cautionary example. Since the 1990s, China accumulated vast amounts of currency reserves, due to the US running a huge trade deficit which ran into hundreds of billions of dollars. With these reserves, China acquired large sums of American debt, keeping their own currency artificially low; in turn this acquisition of US treasuries kept US interest rates artificially low, thus perpetuating the trade cycle. As a result of this relationship, China has maintained a trade surplus and low labour costs, while America lost an estimated 2.7 million jobs to China by 2011. Moreover, China's global reach and influence has been greatly bolstered, not least because they own a significant portion of America's debt. In 2008 the financial crisis, caused by a culture of cheap credit, nearly led to a global financial disaster. In economics, as in everyday life, the effect of creating a something-for-nothing culture of easy credit and cheap goods has proved disastrous in the long run, both

---

[19] Barry Schwartz, The Paradox of Choice: Why More is Less (New York, NY: Harper Perennial, 2005).

for the moral culture of a nation and its economic prosperity.

Ecological policy

Conservation is clearly in the DNA of the conservative tradition. This should extend to the world we live in as much as it does to the just institutions in our societies. The preservation of our native countryside and ultimately our planet ought to be considered of paramount importance. According to the WWF, roughly a quarter of coral reefs around the world are now damaged beyond repair. By some estimates, only 10% of rainforests will be left by the year 2030, at the current rate of deforestation. As a result, there are, at the lowest estimates, between 200 and 2000 species going extinct every year. In the world today there are a host of ecological issues that should cause us grave concern. The response to such issues should be government-led and robust. Simply hoping for the best and allowing the free market to take its course will not suffice. Investment in low carbon energy technologies, tax incentives for ecologically friendly businesses and the creation of multilateral international agreements are all vital steps towards preserving the ecological future of our planet. Conservatives should be the strongest advocates of preserving the natural world.

Architecture

Just as we look to preserve our countryside, so the inheritance given to us in our cities and towns should also be preserved. As John Hayes, the transport minister, recently wrote: 'the overwhelming majority of public architecture built during my lifetime is aesthetically worthless, simply because it is ugly'. It is unsurprising to discover that surveys taken by Yougov and The Prince's Trust discovered that the overwhelming majority of the public preferred architecture that was built in keeping with traditional styles. Sadly, much contemporary architecture seems to show a disdain for public opinion, instead following whatever theory is currently in vogue or the design that returns the highest profits. There can sometimes be an infantilism in contemporary architecture, which seeks simply to shock, or confound the public desire for beauty. As Hayes writes in relation to modern transport architecture, 'There is something profoundly elitist about the way that ugliness has been imposed upon it'. Architecture is distinct from art in one crucial respect – its forms are a part of our public life, and as such, they shape the tone and texture of the world we all live in. In Hayes' view, investors are too often 'eager to associate themselves with the momentary shock of brash novelty', or worse, motivated simply by greed, building 'what is cheap and easy'. It is a sad truth that 'few of the culprits would choose to live or spend their own working lives in the structures they make'. Just as the beauty of past architecture has been left for us to enjoy, so we should seek to bless the generations that follow us with beauty, instead of crudity and shock value.

'To make us love our country, our country ought to be lovely', wrote Edmund Burke in *The Reflections*. In the long run, beautiful architecture is not only an economically sound investment but it brings its own reward for citizens who appreciate its beauty every day. In five hundred years it is likely that the Perpendicular Gothic of Magdalen college, the Baroque of Blenheim Palace, and the Palladian of Stourhead House will stand, long after the legacy of the brutalists, modernists and deconstructivists has crumbled. Christopher Wren, Capability Brown and George Gilbert Scott are names as famous today as they were in their own. Yet forty years on, the names of modern architects have faded from the public imagination. For the conservative, architecture is a medium through which we can lift our thoughts, express the continuity of our history, and understand more of our own story. In this regard, Keats was right in seeing a special kinship between truth and beauty.

Conclusion

In many of their ambitions Burke and Locke were remarkably closely aligned. Both were religious men who sought toleration for religious dissenters and both were seemingly animated by a desire for peace, justice and civil concord. We have seen that where these two great men find themselves in fundamental disagreement is in their conception of man and the state as well as in their methodological approach to politics. We identified that one corollary of Burke's affirmation of the Christian religion as the ground of the state was a belief in the incremental development of the state in accordance with the natural law. We saw that, for Burke, this law was operative in the moral instincts and prudential reason of men. By contrast, Locke believed the state emerged from man's volition. Similarly Locke's conception of man was not rooted in substantive religious doctrines but in the idea of man in the state of nature endowed with subjectively held rights. As we have seen, the Supreme Being of the *Second Treatise* was incidental enough to Locke's political project that the liberal tradition was able to sever God entirely in subsequent formulations of liberal political thought.

Whilst we have looked at length at the theological issues that arise with a political system which is built upon a conception of humans as free and equal, we have seen that the conservative tradition also esteems the ideals of freedom and equality. Burke argued that it was precisely because of the value which the British constitution attributed to freedom and equality that the liberal tradition was gifted with these ideas. We have also heard his belief that if ideas of freedom and equality are to do good and not ill they must always be qualified, limited and couched within a particular context. Burke did not hope to renovate society according to a conception of the individual as naturally free precisely because he believed that this was the surest way to jeopardise the existing freedoms and the equality before the law which British citizens actually enjoyed.

For Christians in the Burkean tradition, the normative standard of freedom and equality is not to be found in an idealised form of man's own reflection, but in the image of Christ. Christians would say that the divine natural law, the revelation of the Bible and the guidance of the Holy Spirit are accessible and can be realised in our flawed human condition. Characteristics of Christ's coming rule are thus appropriated to our own concrete circumstances in just laws and cultures which concede that the final rule is Christ's alone. In this view, tyranny and human suffering are deposed, not on the basis of inherent natural rights, but on the basis of the divine requirement for justice and human dignity. Yet, as Burke well understood, the admission that we still occupy a fallen world necessitates a sensitivity to circumstance, context and prudential judgements in seeking to appropriate right order to our own contexts.

The pursuit of a culture which seeks to uphold Christ's lordship must always be held in tension with the admission that the Kingdom has not yet arrived. Human beings must be allowed the freedom to reject Christ, if they so choose. In response to the argument that a secular liberal democratic state allows just this – a sphere of limited freedom for individuals to accept or reject Christ, a freedom which is limited only by the bounds of property, civil rights and equality – I have sought to make the case that the character of the contractarian liberal state is more substantial than a simple arena of negative freedom in which an objective form of reason dictates the terms of public debate. While liberalism has been publicly presented in such terms, this book has endeavoured to highlight the undergirding axioms and methodological assumptions which animate the liberal tradition. In contrast, Burke and his followers today understand that, if the political ordering of a nation is not to be arbitrary, there must be a distinctive cultural discourse according to which a nation is politically ordered.

While a secular liberal ideology pervades the political discourse of the nation, I have argued with Burke that the firmest foundation for freedom consists in an accurate comprehension of the world through the lens of Christian faith and a preservation of those elements of our cultural and legal landscape that have emerged from this tradition in the British isles.

It has remained a central belief of the Burkean conservative tradition that a rejuvenation of culture in the civil realm, and the operation of prudence in the political realm, are more potent than political theorisation. In the final analysis, it is the decision of the individuals who compose a nation to choose which they will put first, a belief in man, autonomous, equal and a bearer of natural rights, or a belief in Christ, in whom human dignity is redeemed. We have seen that from a Christian theological perspective, the distinctive vocation of the Church is to proclaim the message of the gospel and in doing so transform the culture of a nation. If we are to take the claims of the Christian gospel seriously, then secular politics do not provide a final solution to the strife that attends the co-existence of human beings in a complex world. For politics to know its true vocation and its proper limits, it necessarily requires the Church's proclamation of the true ground upon which all authority rests.

I have argued that at the foundation of the liberal contractarian tradition is an anthropology and an account of secular authority which sits uneasily alongside Christian doctrine, as well as a methodological approach to politics which elevates human reason to the detriment of a more expansive theological account of human sociability. As such, the liberal tradition is one which, at its best, has sincerely sought peace and justice but, at its worst, has assumed an ideological form which has sought to denounce and displace the Christian faith. The conservatism of Edmund Burke provides a more realistic and compassionate approach to human nature, society and therefore politics. In his substantive claims about the nature of humankind, and in the methodological approach to politics which follows from these claims, Burke offers us an old way of approaching new political challenges.

Bibliography

Adams, John, *A defence of the United States of America, against the attacks of m. Turgot in his letter to Dr. Price, dated the twenty-second day of March, 1778*, Vol. I, (London: J. Stockdale, 1794)

Almeida, Joseph, 'Constitutionalism in Burke's *Reflections* as Critique of the Enlightenment Ideas of Originative Political Consent and the Social Compact', *The Catholic Social Science Review*, Vol. 17 (2012) pp. 197-219

Aquinas, Thomas, *Summa Theologica: Prima Secundae Partis*, trans. Fathers of the English Dominican Province, 1920, http://www.newadvent.org/summa/index.html, (accessed 11th March 2014)
-   *De Regno*, trans. Gerald B. Phelan, found at http://dhspriory.org/thomas/DeRegno.htm, (accessed 12th March 2014)

Armitage, David, 'Edmund Burke and Reason of State', *Journal of the History of Ideas*, Vol. 61, Issue 4, pp. 617–34.
-   'John Locke, Carolina and the Two Treatises of Government', *Political Theory*, Vol. 32, No. 5 (2004) pp. 602-627

Ashcraft, Richard, *Locke's Two Treatises of Government* (Abingdon: Routledge, 2010)
-   *Revolutionary Politics and Locke's Two Treatises of Government,* (Princeton, NJ: Princeton University Press, 1986)

Ayling, Stanley, *Edmund Burke: His Life and Opinions* (London: John Murray, 1988)

Baker, J. H., 'St German, Christopher (*c.*1460–1540/41)', *Oxford Dictionary of National Biography*, Oxford University Press, 2004; online edn, Jan 2008, http://www.oxforddnb.com/view/article/24493, (accessed 17th December 2013)

Banner, Michael, 'Christianity and Civil Society', in John A. Coleman (ed.), *Christian Political Ethics* (Princeton, NJ: Princeton University Press, 2007)

Barberá, Pablo, John T. Jost, Jonathan Nagler, Joshua A. Tucker, and Richard Bonneau 'Tweeting From Left to Right: Is Online Political Communication More than an Echo Chamber', in Psychological Science Vol 26, Issue 10, (August, 2015) pp. 1531 – 1542

Barth, Karl, *Church and State* [1938], trans. G. Ronald Howe (London: Smith and Helwys, 2009)

Benedict XVI, *Caritas In Veritate* [Encyclical Letter on Integral Human Development in Charity and Truth], sec. 53, http://w2.vatican.va/content/benedict-xvi/en/encyclicals/documents/hf_benxvi_enc_20090629_caritas-in-veritate.html, (accessed 21st January, 2015)

Berger, P. L., B. Berger, and H. Kellner, *The Homeless Mind: Modernization and Consciousness* (Harmondsworth: Penguin, 1974)

Bernstein, Samuel, *French Political and Intellectual History*, (New Brunswick, NJ: Transaction, 1984)

Biggar, Nigel, *Between Kin and Cosmopolis: An Ethic of the Nation* (Eugene, OR: Cascade, 2014)
- 'The Value of Limited Loyalty: Christianity, the Nation and Territorial Boundaries' in *Christian Political Ethics*, John A. Coleman ed., (Princeton, NJ: Princeton University Press, 2007)
- 'Why the 'establishment' of the Church of England is Good for a Liberal Society', in Mark

Chapman, Judith Maltby, William Whyte (eds.), *The Established Church: Past, Present and Future* (London: T & T Clark, 2011)

Binmore, Ken, *Natural* Justice, (Oxford: Oxford University Press, 2005)

Blair, Tony 'Our Nation's Future: Multiculturalism and integration', speech delivered on 8th December, 2006

Bredvold, Louis I., 'The Invention of the Ethical Calculus' in Richard Foster Jones (ed.), *The Seventeenth Century* (Stanford, CA: Stanford University Press, 1951)

Bromwich, David, *The Intellectual Life of Edmund Burke*, (London: Harvard University Press, 2014)

BIBLIOGRAPHY

Brooks, Christopher W., 'The place of Magna Carta and the Ancient Constitution in SixteenthCentury English Legal Thought', in Ellis Sandoz, *The Roots of Liberty*

Bruce, Steve, *Secularization: In Defence of an Unfashionable Theory* (Oxford: Oxford University Press, 2013)

Buchanan, James, and Gordon Tullock, *The Calculus of Consent* (Ann Arbor, MI: University of Michigan Press, 1965)

Burgh, James, *Political Disquisitions* (London: E. and C. Dilly, 1774)

Burke, Edmund, *The Works of The Right Honourable Edmund Burke,* sixteen volumes (London: C. and J. Rivington, 1826-27)
- 'An Essay Towards an History of the Laws of England' in *The Works of Edmund Burke,* Vol. 5
  (Boston, Charles C. Little & James Brown, 1839)
- 'Indictment of Warren Hastings' in Lewis Copeland, Lawrence W. Lamm and Stephen J. McKenna (eds.), *The World's Greatest Speeches* (USA: Dover, 4th edition, 1999)
- 'Letter from Burke to an unknown person Jan 20, 1791' in M. W. McConnell, 'Establishment and Toleration in Edmund Burke's "Constitution of Freedom"' *The Supreme Court Review* (1995), pp. 393–462
- 'Letter to Richard Burke' in J. C. D. Clark (ed.), *Reflections on the Revolution in France. A Critical Edition* (Stanford University Press, 2001)
- 'Reports from Committee Appointed to Inspect the Lord's Journal' in *The Works of the Right Honorable Edmund Burke Vol. II.* (London: Holdsworth and Ball, 1834)
- 'Speech on Repeal of the Test and Corporation Acts' in *The Speeches of the Right Honourable Edmund Burke in the House of Commons and in Westminster Hall in Four Volumes,* Vol. III, (London: A. Strahan, 1816)
- 'The Debate on the Repeal of the Test and Corporation Acts, March 2nd, 1790', *House of Commons* (London: John Stockdale, 1790)

Canavan, Francis, *Edmund Burke: Prescription and Providence*

(Durham, N.C.: Carolina Academic Press, 1987)

- 'Edmund Burke's Conception of the Role of Reason in Politics' in Iain Hampsher-Monk ed., *Edmund Burke*, (Farnham: Ashgate, 2009)
- *The Political Reason of Edmund Burke*, (Durham, NC: Duke University Press, 1960)

Canning, George, in 'The Anti-Jacobin Review and True Churchman's Magazine', Vol. XLVI, (January to June 1814)

Carey, George, and Andrew Carey, *We Don't do God: The Marginalisation of Public Faith* (Oxford: Monarch Books, 2012)

Casey, Louise, 'The Casey Review: A review into opportunity and integration', https://www.gov.uk/government/uploads/system/uploads/attachment_data/file/575973/The_Casey_Review_Report.pdf (accessed 20th January, 2017)

Churchill, Winston, 'Consistency in Politics' [1932] in James W. Muller (ed.) *Thoughts and Adventures: Churchill Reflects on Spies, Cartoons, Flying and the Future* (Wilmington, DE: ISI, 2009)

Clark, J. C. D., 'Religious Affiliation and Dynastic Allegiance in Eighteenth-Century England: Edmund Burke, Thomas Paine and Samuel Johnson', *English Literary History*, Vol. 64, Issue 4, pp. 1029–67

- (ed.), *Reflections on the Revolution in France: A Critical Edition* (Stanford, CA: Stanford University Press, 2001)
- *The Language of Liberty*, (Cambridge: Cambridge University Press, 1994)

Cobban, Alfred, *Edmund Burke and the Revolt against the Eighteenth Century: A Study of the Political and Social Thinking of Burke, Wordsworth, Coleridge and Southey*, (London: Ruskin House, 1929)

Coke, Edward, *Coke Report 8.*

- 'Case of Proclamations', found at 'England and Wales High Court (King's Bench Division) Decisions', http://www.bailii.org/ew/cases/EWHC/KB/1610/J22.html, (accessed 13th January 2014)
- 'Calvin's Case', found at 'The Constitution Society',

BIBLIOGRAPHY

http://www.constitution.org/coke/Calvins_Case-7_Coke_ Report_1a_77_ER_377.html, (accessed 20th December 2013)

Coleridge, Samuel T., *On the Constitution of the Church and State* [1826] (Charleston, SC: Nabu Press, 2012)

Colman, John, *John Locke's Moral Philosophy* (Edinburgh: Edinburgh University Press, 1983)

Crepell, Ingrid, *Toleration and Identity: Foundations in Early Modern Thought* (Abingdon: Routledge, 2003)

Cromartie, Alan, *Sir Matthew Hale, 1609-1676: Law, Religion and Natural Philosophy* (Cambridge: Cambridge University Press, 1995)

Cruise O'Brien, Conor, *The Great Melody: A Thematic Biography of Edmund Burke* (Chicago: University of Chicago Press, 1994)

Dawson, Christopher, in *The Portable Conservative Reader*, ed. Russell Kirk (New York, NY: Penguin, 1982)

Deane, Seamus, *The French Revolution and Enlightenment in England* (London: Harvard University Press, 1988)

Descartes, René, *The Method, Meditations, and Selections from the Principles,* trans. John Veitch, (Edinburgh, W. Blackwood & Sons, 6th edition, 1879)

D'Alembert, Jean Le Rond, *Preliminary Discourse*, Vol. I, trans. Richard N. Schwab and Walter E. Rex, (Indianapolis, IN: Bobbs-Merrill, 1963)

D'Holbach, Baron, *Elements de la Morale Universelle, ou Catechism Universelle,* trans. Mitch Abador, found at www.marxists.org/reference/ archive/holbach/1765/catechism.htm, (accessed, February 12th, 2014)

Dickinson, H. T., *British Radicalism & The French Revolution 1789-1815* (Oxford: Basil Blackwell, 1985)

Donahue, Jr, Charles, 'Roman Canon Law in the Medieval English Church: Stubbs v Maitland Reexamined', *Michigan Law Review*, Vol. 72, No. 4, (Mar., 1974)

Donlan, Sean Patrick, 'Law and Lawyers in Edmund Burke's Scottish Enlightenment', *Studies in Burke and His Time*, Vol. 20, No. 1, (2005)

Doyle, William, *Oxford History of the French Revolution*, (Oxford: Oxford University Press, 2nd edition, 2002)

Dunn, John, *The Political Thought of John Locke: An Historical Account of the Argument of the 'Two Treatises of Government'* (Cambridge: Cambridge University Press, 1969)
-   'The Politics of Locke in England and America', in John Dunn (ed.) *Political Obligation in its Historical Context* (Cambridge, 1980)

Dustmann, Christian, Albrecht Glitz and Tommaso Frattinip, 'The Labour Market Impact of Immigration', Oxford Review of Economic Policy, Vol. 24, Number 3, (2008) pp. 477-494. p. 491.

Eliot, T. S., *Notes towards the Definition of Culture* (London: Faber and Faber, 2nd edition 1962)
-   *The Idea of a Christian Society* (New York, NY: Harcourt, Brace, 1939)

Field, Clive, 'Counting Religion in England and Wales: The Long Eighteenth Century, c. 1680- c.1840', *Journal of Ecclesiastical History*, Vol. 63., No. 4, October 2012, pp. 693-720.

Figgis, John, *Churches in the Modern State* (London, 1913)

Fortescue, John, 'De Natura Legis Naturae', in *The Works of Sir John Fortescue Knight, Chief Justice of England and Lord Chancellor to King Henry VI.* Vol. i. (London: Chiswick Press, 1869)
-   *De Laudibus Legum Angliae* (Cambridge: J. Smith, 1825)

Freeman, Samuel, *Justice and the Social Contract* (Oxford: Oxford University Press, 2007)

Ghautier, David, *Morals by Agreement* (Oxford: Clarendon Press, 1986)

Gliozzo, Charles A., 'The Philosophes and Religion: Intellectual Origins of the Dechristianization Movement in the French Revolution' *Church History*, Vol. 40, No. 3 (Sep., 1971) pp. 273-283.

Grant, Ruth, *John Locke's Liberalism* (London: University of Chicago Press, 1987)

Greenfield Adams, Randolph, *Political Ideas of the American Revolution*, (New York: Barnes and Noble, 1939)

Gregory, Brad, *Salvation at Stake: Christian Martyrdom in Early Modern* Europe (Cambridge, MA: Harvard University Press, 1999)

Grotius, Hugo, *De jure belli ac pacis libri tres,* Prolegomena, II, trans. Francis W. Kelsey in *The Classics of International Law,* ed. J. B. Scott, (Oxford, Clarendon Press, 1925)

Halévy, Elie, *The Growth of Philosophic Radicalism*, (New York, NY: The Macmillan Company, 1928) Hampsher-Monk, Iain, 'Burke and the Religious Sources of Skeptical Conservatism', in *Edmund Burke*, ed. Iain Hampsher-Monk (Farnham: Ashgate, 2009)
  - 'Reflections on the Revolution in France', in David Dwan and Christopher Insole, (eds.), *The Cambridge Companion to Edmund Burke,* (Cambridge: Cambridge University Press, 2012) *Hansard's Parliamentary History*, 21 (London: T. C. Hansard, 1814)

Harris, Ian, 'Burke and Religion' in Christopher Insole and David Dwan, (eds.), *The Cambridge Companion to Edmund Burke,* (Cambridge: Cambridge University Press, 2012)

Hauerwas, Stanley, *After Christendom* (Nashville, TN: Abingdon Press, 2nd Edition 1999)
  - *Resident Aliens: Life in the Christian Colony* (Nashville, TN: Abingdon Press, 1989)
  - *The Peaceable Kingdom: A Primer in Christian Ethics* (London: SCM, 2003)

Helmholz, R. H., 'Continental Law and Common Law: Historical Strangers or Companions?', *Duke Law Journal*, Vol. 6., (December 1990) pp. 1207-1228
  - *Roman Canon Law in Reformation England* (Cambridge: Cambridge University Press, 2004)

Hitchens, Peter, *The Rage Against God: Why Faith is the Foundation of Civilisation* (London: Continuum, 2010); Michael Nazir-Ali, *Triple Jeopardy for the West*, (London: Bloomsbury, 2012)

Hobbes, Thomas, *De Cive*, (London: J.C. for R. Royston, 1651)

- *Leviathan*, ed. Richard Tuck (Cambridge: Cambridge University Press, 1991) Hobsbawn, Eric, *The Age of Revolution: 1789-1848* (London: Abacus, 1962)

Hoffman, Ross, and Paul Levack, *Burke's Politics* (New York, NY: Alfred A. Knopf, 1949)

Holdsworth, W. S., *Sources and Literature of English Law*, (Oxford: Clarendon Press, 1925)

Hooker, Richard, *Of the Laws of Ecclesiastical Polity*, Vol. I, ed. Stephen McGrade (Oxford: Oxford University Press, 2013)

Hordern, Joshua, *Political Affections: Civic Participation and Moral Theology* (Oxford: Oxford University Press, 2013)

Horton, John, and Susan Mendus, *John Locke: A Letter Concerning Toleration in Focus* (London: Routledge, 1991)

'House of Reps. Of Mass. To Conway', [Feb. 13, 1768], Almon, *Prior Documents*, pp. 181-2. Quoted in Randolph Greenfield Adams, *Political Ideas of the American Revolution*, (New York: Barnes and Noble, 1939)

House of Lords, Select Committee on Economic Affairs, 1st Report of Session 2007-08 'The Economic Impact of Immigration' Vol. I Report, https://www.publications.parliament.uk/pa/ld200708/ldselect/ldeconaf/82/82.pdf (accessed 3rd February, 2017)

Howell, Ronald, 'A Review of The Political Reason of Edmund Burke by Francis P. Canavan', *The Journal of Politics* 22 (1960) pp. 730–732

Hughes, John, 'After Temple? The Recent Renewal of Anglican Social Thought', in *Anglican Social Theology: Renewing the Vision Today*, ed. Malcom Brown, (London: Church House Publishing, 2014)

Hutcheson, Francis, *An Inquiry into the Original of our Ideas of Beauty and Virtue: in two treatises. I. Concerning Beauty, Order, Harmony, Design II. Concerning Moral Good and Evil* (London: 3rd edition, 1729)

Insole, Christopher, 'Burke and the Natural Law' in David Dwan and Christopher Insole (eds.), *The Cambridge Companion to Edmund Burke,* (Cambridge: Cambridge University Press, 2012)
- 'Two Conceptions of Liberalism' in *Journal of Religious Ethics*, Vol. 36. Issue 3, pp. 447-489. p. 452.

Israel, Jonathan I., *Radical Enlightenment: Philosophy and the Making of Modernity 1650-1750* (Oxford: Oxford University Press, 2001)
- *Revolutionary Ideas: An Intellectual History of the French Revolution from The Rights of Man to Robespierre* (Princeton, NJ: Princeton University Press, 2014)

Ives, E. W., 'Fortescue, Sir John (*c.*1397–1479)', *Oxford Dictionary of National Biography*, Oxford University Press, 2004; online edn, Oct 2005, http://www.oxforddnb.com/view/article/9944, (accessed 17th December 2013)

Jacobs, E. F., 'Sir John Fortescue and the Law of Nature', *Bulletin of the John Ryland Library*, Vol. 18, No.2, (July, 1934)

Jefferson, Thomas, 'Letter to James Madison, Sep. 6, 1789' in *The Papers of Thomas Jefferson*, ed. Julian P. Boyd, (Princeton, NJ: Princeton University Press, 1950)
- Jefferson 'Letter to Diodati, 3rd August 1789', *Papers*, XV

Kant, Immanuel, *Critique of Practical Reason*, ed. Mary J. Gregor (Cambridge: Cambridge University Press, 1997)

Kirk, Russell, *Edmund Burke: A Genius Reconsidered* (New York, NY: Arlington House, 1967)
- 'Ten Conservative Principles', http://www.kirkcenter.org/index.php/detail/tenhttp://www.kirkcenter.org/index.php/detail/ten-conservative-principles/conservative-principles/, (accessed 22nd October 2013)

Lafayette, "Sur la declaration des droits," Memoires, II, 303-4, in Margaret Madox and Louis Reichenthal Gottschalk, 'Lafayette in the French Revolution, through the October days' (Chicago, IL: University of Chicago Press, 1973)

Laslett, Peter, *Two Treatises of Government*, (Cambridge: Cambridge University Press, 1988)

Leo XIII, *Rerum Novarum*, [Encyclical Letter on Capital and Labour], sec. 32, http://w2.vatican.va/content/leo-xiii/en/encyclicals/documents/hf_l-xiii_enc_15051891_rerumhttp://w2.vatican.va/content/leo-xiii/en/encyclicals/documents/hf_l-xiii_enc_15051891_rerum-novarum.htmlnovarum.html, (accessed 21st January, 2015)

Lester, John H., 'An Analysis of the Conservative Thought of Edmund Burke', Ph.D. Thesis, Harvard University, 1943

Lewis, C. S., 'Is Theology Poetry' in *The Weight of Glory: And Other Addresses* (New York, NY: 1949, HarperCollins)

Lock, F. P., *Edmund Burke II, 1784–1797* (Oxford: Oxford University Press, 2006)

Locke, John, *An Essay Concerning Human Understanding*, [1689], ed. Kenneth P. Winkler, (Cambridge: Hackett, 1996)
- *A Letter Concerning Toleration* (Huddersfield: J. Brook, 1796)
- *Political* Essays, ed. Mark Goldie (New York, NY: Cambridge University Press, 1997)
- *Two Treatises on Government* [1690] ed. Peter Laslett, (Cambridge: Cambridge University Press, student edition 1988)
- 'Second Treatise of Government', [1690], ed. C.B. Macpherson, (Indianapolis, IN: Hackett, 1980)

House of Lords, Select Committee on Economic Affairs, 1st Report of Session 2007-08 'The Economic Impact of Immigration' Vol. I Report, https://www.publications.parliament.uk/pa/ld200708/ldselect/ldeconaf/82/82.pdf, (accessed 3rd February, 2017) p. 58.

Lough, John, *The Philosophes and Post-Revolutionary France* (Oxford: Clarendon Press, 1982)

Luckmann, T., *The Invisible Religion: The Problem of Religion in Modern Society* (NY: Macmillan, 1967)

MacCunn, John, *The Political Philosophy of Burke*, (New York, NY: Longmans Green and Company; London: Edward Arnold, 1913)

Maciag, Drew, *Edmund Burke in America: The Contested Career of the Father of Modern Conservatism* (Ithaca, NY: Cornell University Press, 2013)

MacIntrye, Alasdair, *After Virtue: A Study in Moral Theory* (Notre Dame, IN: University of Notre Dame Press, 3rd Edition, 2007)

Macleod, Adam, 'A Review of Jean Porter's Ministers of the Law', *The Journal of Faith and the Academy*, Volume IV, Number 1 (Spring, 2011)

Macpherson, C. B., 'Edmund Burke' in Iain Hampsher-Monk (ed.), *Edmund Burke*, (Farnham: Ashgate, 2009)
- *Burke* (Oxford: Oxford University Press, 1988)

Maitland, F., *Roman Canon Law in the Church of England: Six* Essays, (London: Methuen, 1898)

Marsh, John, *The Liberal Delusion: The Roots of our Current Moral Crisis* (Bury St. Edmunds: Arena Books, 2012)

Milbank, John, *Theology and Social Theory: Beyond Secular Reason* (Oxford: Blackwell, 1990)

Milbank, John, Catherine Pickstock and Graham Ward, *Radical Orthodoxy: A New Theology* (London: Routledge, 1999)

Mitchell, L. G., 'Fox, Charles James (1749–1806)', *Oxford Dictionary of National Biography*, Oxford University Press, 2004; online edn, Oct 2007, http://www.oxforddnb.com/view/article/10024, (accessed 29 April 2013)

Morley, John, *Edmund Burke: A Historical Study* (London, 1867)

Murphy, Jessica, 'Toronto professor Jordan Petersen takes on gender neutral pronouns', http://www.bbc.co.uk/news/world-us-canada-37875695, (accessed 15th January 2017)

Nazir-Ali, Michael, *Triple Jeopardy for the West*, (London: Bloomsbury, 2012)

Niebuhr, Reinhold, *Moral Man and Immoral Society: A Study in Ethics and Politics* [1932] (London: Westminster John Knox Press, 2001)

Niemeyer, Gerhart, 'Russell Kirk and Ideology', *The InterCollegiate Review*, Vol. 30 (Fall, 1994) pp. 35-38

Nussbaum, Martha, 'Perfectionist Liberalism and Political Liberalism', *Philosophy and Public Affairs*, Vol. 39, Issue 1, (Winter, 2011) pp. 3-45

O'Donovan, Oliver, *Bonds of Imperfection,* (Grand Rapids, MI: Eerdmans, 2004) - *Resurrection and Moral Order* (Grand Rapids: MI: Eerdmans, 2nd Edition, 1994)
- *The Desire of the Nations: Rediscovering the Roots of Political Theology* (Cambridge: Cambridge University Press, 1996)
- *The Ways of Judgement* (Cambridge: Eerdmans, 2005)

O'Donovan, Oliver and Joan Lockwood O'Donovan, *From Irenaeus to Grotius: A Sourcebook in Christian Political Thought* (Cambridge: Eerdmanns, 2000)

O'Neill, Onora, 'Constructivism in Rawls and Kant', in Samuel Richard Freeman (ed.) *The Cambridge Companion to Rawls*, (Cambridge: Cambridge University Press, 2003)

O'Sullivan, K. C., Richard, 'Natural Law and Common Law', *Transaction of the Grotius Society,* Vol. 31, (1945). pp. 117-138

Page, Anthony, *John Jebb and the Enlightenment Origins of British Radicalism* (London: Praeger, 2003)

Pappin III, Joseph, 'Edmund Burke's Progeny: Recent Scholarship on Burke's Political Philosophy', *Political Science Reviewer*, Vol. 35 (2006)

Perry, John, *The Pretences of Loyalty* (Oxford: Oxford University Press, 2011)

Pius IX, *Quadragesimo Anno* Encyclical Letter on Reconstruction of the Social Order, sec. 122, http://w2.vatican.va/content/pius-xi/en/encyclicals/documents/hf_phttp://w2.vatican.va/content/pius-xi/en/encyclicals/documents/hf_p-xi_enc_19310515_quadragesimo-anno.htmlxi_enc_19310515_quadragesimo-anno.html, (accessed 21st January, 2015)

Pocock, J. G. A., *Politics, Language and Time: Essays on Political Thought and History* (Chicago: University of Chicago Press, 1971)
- *The Machiavellian Moment: Florentine Political Thought and the Atlantic Republican Tradition* (Princeton, NJ: Princeton University Press, 1975)

Polasky, Janet, *Revolutions Without Borders: The Call to Liberty in the Atlantic World* (New Haven, CT: Yale University Press, 2015)

Pollock, F. and F. Maitland, *The History of English Law before the time of Edward I*, (Cambridge: Cambridge University Press, 2nd edition, 1911)

Prest, Wilfred, *Albion Ascendant: English History 1660-1815* (New York, NY: Oxford University Press, 1998)

Price, Polly J., 'Natural Law and Birthright Citizenship in Calvin's Case (1608)', *Yale Journal of Law and the Humanities,* Vol. 9, Issue 1, Article 2 (2013) pp. 73-143

Price, Richard, 'A Discourse on the Love of Our Country' [1790], in Ellis Sandoz ed., *Political Sermons of the American Founding Era: 1730-1805,* Vol. 2 (2nd Ed. Indianapolis: Liberty Fund, 1998)

Rahner, Karl, "Ideology and Christianity," *Theological Investigations,* trans. Karl-H. and Boniface Krueger (Baltimore: Helicon, 1969)

Ramsay, Maureen, *What's Wrong With Liberalism? A Radical Critique of Liberal Political Philosophy* (London: Leicester University Press, 1997)

Rand, R. K., *Cicero in the Courtroom of St. Thomas Aquinas* (Milwaukee, WI: Marquette University Press, 1946) p. 4

Randall, John H., *The Making of the Modern Mind*, (Boston, MA: Houghton Mifflin, 1940)

Rawls, John, *A Theory of Justice* (Cambridge, MA: Harvard University Press, 1971)
- *A Theory of Justice* (Cambridge MA: Harvard University Press, revised edition 1999)
- *Justice as Fairness: A Restatement*, ed. Erin Kelly (Cambridge, MA: Harvard University Press, 2001)

- 'Kantian Constructivism in Moral Theory', *Journal of Philosophy*, 77 (1980) pp. 515–572
- *Lectures on the History of Moral Philosophy*, ed. Barbara Herman (Cambridge, MA: Harvard University Press, 2000)
- 'The Idea of an Overlapping Consensus', *Philosophical Papers,* ed. J. Freeman, (Cambridge MA: Harvard University Press, 1999)

'Rawls Remembered', in *The Philosophy Magazine*, Issue 22, 2003, p.34

Rensin, Emmit, 'The Smug Style in American Liberalism', http://www.vox.com/2016/4/21/11451378/smug-american-liberalism (accessed February 18th, 2017)

Revolution Society, The, *The New Annual Register, Or General Repository of History, Politics, And Literature for the Year 1789* (London: J. Robinson, 1790)

Robespierre, Maximilien, *Lettres à ses Commettans*, Vol. 2, (January 5th, 1793)

Rousseau, Jean-Jacques, *The Social Contract* [1762], ed. Tom Griffith, (London: Wordsworth Editions, 1998)

Sacks, Jonathan, 'Giving and belonging: The lesson Jews can offer new immigrants', http://rabbisacks.org/giving-and-belonging-the-lesson-jews-can-offer-new-immigrants/ (accessed 21st January, 2017)

Sandel, Michael, *Liberalism and the Limits of Justice*, (Cambridge: Cambridge University Press, 2nd edition, 1998)

Sandoz, Ellis, *The Politics of Truth and Other Untimely Essays: The Crisis of Civic Consciousness* (Columbia, MI: University of Missouri Press, 1999)
- *The Roots of Liberty: Magna Carta, Ancient Constitution, and the Anglo-American Tradition of Rule of Law* (Columbia, MO: University of Missouri Press, 1993)

Scattola, Merio, 'Before and After Natural Law: Models of Natural Law in Ancient and Modern Times', in Tim Hochstrasser and Paul

Schröder, (eds.), *Early Modern Natural Law Theories: Context and Strategies in the Early Enlightenment* (Boston: Kluwer, 2003)

Scott, Matthew http://www.telegraph.co.uk/news/2016/05/11/trigger-warnings-at-oxford-would-threaten-academic-freedom-and-i/, (accessed 21st February, 2017)

Schwartz, Barry, *The Paradox of Choice: Why More is Less* (New York, NY: Harper Perennial, 2005)

Schwartzman, Micah, 'The Relevance of Locke's Religious Arguments for Toleration' *Political Theory*, Vol. 33, No. 5 (2005) pp. 678-705

Scruton, Roger, 'Man's Second Disobedience: a Vindication of Burke' in Iain Hampsher-Monk ed., *Edmund Burke*, (Farnham: Ashgate, 2009)
- *The Meaning of Conservatism* (Basingstoke: Palgrave, 2001)
- 'Why I Became a Conservative' in *The Roger Scruton Reader*, ed. Mark Dooley (London: Continuum, 2009)

Seipp, David J., 'The Reception of Canon Law and Civil Law in the Common Law Courts before 1600', *Oxford Journal of Legal Studies*, Vol. 13, No. 3 (Autumn, 1993) pp. 388-420

Selden, John, *England's Epinomis*, (London: Thomas Basset and Richard Chiswell, 1683)
- *Of the Dominion, or, Ownership of the Sea*, trans. Marchamont Nedham (London, William Du Gard, 1652)
- *Opera Omnia,* Vol. III, cols. 1891-2, quoted in Richard Tuck, *Natural Rights Theories* (Cambridge: Cambridge University Press, 1979)
- *Table Talk,* (1689) (Oxford: Clarendon Press, 1992)

Sissons, Peter, quoted in 'Left Wing Bias? It's written through the BBC's very DNA, says Peter Sissons', http://www.dailymail.co.uk/news/article-1349506/Left-wing-bias-Its-written-BBCs-DNA-says-Peter-Sissons.html (accessed 15th February, 2017)

Song, Robert, *Christianity and Liberal Society*, (Oxford: Oxford University Press, 2006)

St. Germain, Christopher, *The Dialogue in English, betweene a Doctor of Divinity, and a Student in the Laws of England*, (John More, 1638)

Stanlis, Peter, *Edmund Burke and the Natural Law* (Lafayette: Huntington House, 1986)
- 'Edmund Burke's Legal Erudition and Practical Politics: Ireland and the American Revolution', *The Political Science Reviewer*, Vol. 35, Number 1, Fall 2006
- 'The Basis of Burke's Political Conservatism', *Modern Age,* (Summer 1961) pp. 263-265
- *The Best of Burke: Selected Writings and Speeches of Edmund Burke*, Peter J. Stanlis ed., (Washington D.C.: Regnery, 1963)
- *The Enlightenment and Revolution* (London: Transaction, 1991)

Stein, Peter, 'Continental Influences on English Legal Thought, 1600-1900', in *The Character and Influence of the Roman Civil Law: Historical Essays,* ed. Peter Stein (London: Hambledon, 1988)

Stephen, Leslie, *History of English Thought in the Eighteenth Century*, Vol. II (London, 1881)

Strauss, *Natural Right and History* (Chicago IL: University of Chicago Press, 1963)

Tacitus, *Germania,* found at 'Fordham University Medieval Sourcebook', http://www.fordham.edu/halsall/source/tacitus1.html, (accessed 5th March 2014)

Taylor Wilkins, Burleigh, *The Problem of Burke's Political Philosophy*, (Oxford: Oxford University Press, 1967)

Temple, William, *Christianity and Social Order* (London: SCM Press, 1950)

Thomas, D. O., 'Price, Richard (1723–1791)', *Oxford Dictionary of National Biography*, Oxford University Press, 2004; online edn, May 2005, http://www.oxforddnb.com/view/article/22761, (accessed 2nd May 2013)

Tuck, Richard, *Natural Rights Theories* (Cambridge: Cambridge University Press, 1979)
- Tuck, 'The "modern" theory of natural law', in *The Languages of Political Theory in Early Modern Europe*, ed. Anthony Pagden (Cambridge: Cambridge University Press, 1987)

Turner, Ralph V., 'Roman law in England before the time of Bracton', *Journal of British Studies,* Vol. 15, No. 1 (Autumn, 1975)

von Leyden, W., *Hobbes and Locke: The Politics of Freedom and Obligation* (London: Macmillan, 1981)
- 'Locke and Natural Law' in *Philosophy*, Vol. 31, No. 116 (1956) pp. 23-35

Waldron, Jeremy, *God, Locke and Equality,* (Cambridge: Cambridge University Press, 2002)

Welsby, W. N., ed., *Lives of Eminent English of the Seventeenth and Eighteenth Centuries* (London: W. M'Dowall, 1846)

West, Ed, *The Diversity Illusion: What We Got Wrong about Immigration and How to Set it Right* (UK: Gibson Square, 2013) p. 88.

Whitney, Lois, *Primitivism and the Idea of Progress* (Baltimore: Johns Hopkins Press, 1934)

Wolff, Robert Paul, *Understanding Rawls: A Reconstruction and Critique of a Theory of Justice* (Princeton: Princeton University Press, 1977)

Ziskind, Martha A., 'John Selden: Criticism and Affirmation of the Common Law Tradition' *The American Journal of Legal History*, Vol. 19., No. 1 (Jan., 1975) pp. 22-39

Zuckert, Michael, 'The Fullness of Being: Thomas Aquinas and the Modern Critique of Natural Law', *The Review of Politics*, Vol. 69, No. 1 (Winter, 2007) pp. 28-47

About the Author

Samuel Burgess studied at the University of Durham, where he received a Vice-Chancellor's scholarship and a first class degree in theology. He subsequently studied for an M.Phil at the University of Cambridge and a D.Phil at the University of Oxford. He is a former Kluge Fellow at the Library of Congress and has tutored in Christian ethics.